POETRY COMPE

GREAT MINDS

Your World...Your Future...YOUR WORDS

From Co Durham
Edited by Steve Twelvetree

First published in Great Britain in 2005 by:
Young Writers
Remus House
Coltsfoot Drive
Peterborough
PE2 9JX
Telephone: 01733 890066
Website: www.youngwriters.co.uk

All Rights Reserved

© Copyright Contributors 2005

SB ISBN 1 84460 718 6

Foreword

This year, the Young Writers' 'Great Minds' competition proudly presents a showcase of the best poetic talent selected from over 40,000 up-and-coming writers nationwide.

Young Writers was established in 1991 to promote the reading and writing of poetry within schools and to the youth of today. Our books nurture and inspire confidence in the ability of young writers and provide a snapshot of poems written in schools and at home by budding poets of the future.

The thought, effort, imagination and hard work put into each poem impressed us all and the task of selecting poems was a difficult but nevertheless enjoyable experience.

We hope you are as pleased as we are with the final selection and that you and your family continue to be entertained with *Great Minds From Co Durham* for many years to come.

Contents

Carmel RC Technology College

Charlotte McAuley (13)	1
Rebecca Eldrington (13)	2
William Jones (13)	2
Mark Delaney (14)	3
Katie Oxley (13)	4
Thomas Stokell (13)	4
Elizabeth Sutcliffe (13)	5
James Potts (11)	5
Thomas Wilson (11)	6
Sophie Mackay (13)	6
Patrick Wharton (13)	7
Abbi Fluen (14)	7
Becca Webber (11)	8
Rachel Musgrave (13)	8
Samantha Gardiner (14)	9
Liam Coates (13)	10
Bethany Harper (11)	10
Theo Lyonette (11)	11
Ross Kelly (13)	11
Hannah Miller (13)	12
Alice Daniel (11)	12
Laura Blake (13)	13
Kirsty Coleman (13)	13
Charlotte Lancaster (13)	14
Paul McDermott (11)	14
Thomas Haile (13)	15
Neil Hanlon (11)	15
Natasha Redpath (12)	16
Louise Sowerby (11)	16
Kay Hardisty (12)	17
Laura Myers (12)	17
Andrew Jordan (12)	18
Sophie Norman (11)	18
Hannah Gohr (12)	19
Melissa Sample (12)	20
Robyn Ward (11)	20
Lorna Goldsmith (12)	21
Rebecca King (11)	21

Adam Davison (12)	22
Victoria Mackenzie (14)	22
Alisha Sinha (13)	23
Nicola Bleasby (12)	23
Darren Swankie (13)	24
Christina Muller (13)	24
Michael Thurloway (12)	25
Richard McAllister (12)	26
Rachael Peeke (14)	26
Sam Jinks (11)	27
Christopher Ward (12)	27
Leah Kennedy (11)	28
Jade Towse (13)	28
Robert Corless (12)	29
Kieren Kemp (13)	29
Kyrie Hunter (14)	30
Sadie McCartney (12)	30
Kate Barker (15)	31
Thomas Ward (13)	31
Steven Brack (12)	32
Paul Jefferson (12)	32
Bethany Heard (15)	33
Chris Kelly (14)	33
Sophie Daniel (14)	34
James Dixon (13)	34
Sarah McDonogh (14)	35
Calum Fovargue (12)	35
Adam Sadler (14)	36
Amy Raper (11)	36
Daniel Fox (15)	37
Jack Ridley (14)	37
Michael Ringwood (13)	38
Sam Robinson (14)	38
Clare Charman (14)	39
Rachel Baines (11)	39
Jonathan Way (14)	40
Christopher Clinton (15)	40
Emma Bantleman (13)	41
Kelly Bravey (14)	41
Chris Richardson (13)	42
Lauren Morgan (14)	43
Stephanie Metcalfe (12)	43

Dean Goldsborough (13)	44
Emma Spraggon (12)	45
Sinead Wisker (13)	46
Stacey Clegg (14)	47
Troy McCaskill (14)	48
David O'Neill (13)	49

Haughton Community School

Fay Austin (11)	49
Ehlana Foley (12)	50
Jayne Blackburn (11)	50
Eve Richardson (12)	51
Shaun MacKenzie (11)	51
Sofia Rustico (13)	52
Georgina Lloyd (13)	52
Lisa McCormick (12)	53
Nicole Marsh (11)	53
Nicola Hedley (12)	54
Callum Crackett (11)	54
Jessica McEwan (12)	55
Abby Peverley (12)	55
Charlie Prendergast (12)	56
Amy Foster & Emma Abernethy (13)	56
Pauline Finney (12)	57
Ellis Hemmings (12)	57
Laura Pearson (12)	58
Kaleigh-Ann Swales (12)	58
Nicola Lodge (12)	59
Hayley Allen (12)	59
Zoe Thompson (12)	60
Elizabeth Raper (13)	60
Charlotte Hall (12)	61
Danielle Ward (14)	61
Jane Armer (12)	62
Matthew Glenning (12)	62
Laura Pinder (12)	63
Jonathon Tweddle (13)	63
Shamila Rahman (13)	64
Liam Browne (11)	64
Hayley Hardman (11)	65
Sara Dobson (11)	65

Philip Bayles (11)	65
Samantha Herrington (13)	66
Karl Wake (11)	66
Daniel Barber (13)	66
Kathryn Smith (13)	67
Hannah Holden (11)	67
Scott Banner (14)	67
Natasha Campbell (12)	68
Amanda Dixon (11)	68
Jamie-Ann Donald (12)	69
Craig Hart (13)	69
Carl Hardman (12)	70
Gareth McShane (14)	70
Amy Foster (12)	71
Hayley Brady (13)	71
Annabel Townsend (11)	72
Rebecca Mills (13)	72
Amy Wearmouth (14)	72
Christina Hauxwell (13)	73
Mark Hall (13)	73
Nicole Atkins (13)	74
Billy Mee (13)	74
Ben Reidy (13)	75
Kara Reed (13)	75
Terri Stephens (11)	76
Craig Stephens (13)	76
Jessica Sandiford (11)	77
Samantha Colbeck (11)	77
Matthew Wain (12)	78
Rebekah Morgan (11)	78
Nikita McNiff (11)	79
Richard Holt (13)	79
Samantha Beckham (11)	80
Natalie Taylor (14)	80
Becky Stephenson (11)	81
Dean McShane (12)	81
Jenna Bell (13)	82
Joe Lythe (12)	82
Lauren Risbrough (11)	82
Kerry Sweeten (14)	83
Sarah Greaves (13)	83
Stephanie Bene (12)	84

Kimberley Stokes (12)   84
Scott Barraclough (12)   85
Stacey Brocklebank (11)   85
William Parkinson (14)   86

Hurworth School - Maths & Computing College
Siân Sunley (13)   86
Rhys Whitney (13)   87
Jessica Kelly (13)   87
Rebecca Ann Edwards (11)   88
Sophie Carvell (11)   88
Laura Carter (12)   89
Chris Smith (12)   90
Melissa Causer (11)   90
Laura Crawford (12)   91
Gemma Eddy (12)   91
Sabriye Wallis (13)   92
Lee Marshall (11)   92
Lauren Mitchell (14)   93
Jennifer Mitchell (13)   93
Chris Oakley (14)   94
Christina Naylor (12)   94
Stuart Read (12)   95
Jack Heseltine (12)   95
Lewis Longstaff (11)   96
Megan Keen (13)   96
Stephen Duncan (13)   97
Jade Hall (13)   97
Jenna Hutchinson (13)   98
Jonathan Weeks   98
Andrew Sanderson (13)   99
Hannah Barron (12)   100
Alexander Glasper (12)   100
Catherine Hodgson (13)   101
Sarah Kitching (12)   102
Jonathan Snowden (13)   102
Sophie Miller (12)   103
Adam Walton (12)   103
Joshua Brennan (12)   104
Brogan May Hendry (12)   105
Vicky Ramsden   106

Sian Hill (12)	106
Elizabeth Doubleday (12)	107
Michael Gowling (12)	107
Sabrina Baker (12)	108
Christopher Fitzgerald (12)	108
Ryan Colling (12)	109
Joanne Bartlett (13)	109
Natalie Lawson (12)	110
Matthew Hall (12)	110
Gillian Akers (14)	111
Emma Jameson (14)	111
Melissa Wheelhouse (12)	112
Oliver Wendel (12)	112
Clare Holme (14)	113
Rebecca Boyd (14)	113
Bobbie Sewell (13)	114
Gemma Baker (13)	114
Chris Lapping (14)	115
James Rickards (12)	116
Aaron Yeomans (13)	116
Colleen Halstead (11)	117
Martin Black (13)	117
Francesca Heath (13)	118
Armarni Cornforth (13)	118
Abigail Jones (13)	119
Michael Myers (11)	119
Joanne Haywood (13)	120
Cameron Dulston (14)	120
Amy Wilson (13)	121
Adrian Balmer (12)	121
Sean Fowler (13)	122
Nathan Bickerton (11)	122
Kelly Ward (11)	123
Lily Hamilton (12)	123
Lauren Burton (12)	124
Craig Robinson (12)	125
Fiona Hamilton (12)	126
Victoria Osborne (12)	126
Ashleigh Hall (12)	127
Robert Forster (13)	127
Lesley Medland (12)	127
Ben Harper (13)	128

Joanna Dinsdale (14)	129
Becky Mullett (13)	130
Rachel Dauber (13)	130
Carl Jameson (13)	131
Catherine Morton (14)	131
Nichola Bateman (13)	132
Robyn Simpson (13)	132
Clare Eddy (13)	133
Tom Flynn (13)	133
Chloë Carlton (11)	134
Beth Frankland (13)	134
Joshua Crane (13)	135
Richard Minto (13)	135
Clare Rudd (13)	136

Lord Lawson Of Beamish School

Danielle Sharkey (11)	136
Craig Atherton (13)	137
Naomi Lea (11)	138
Alex Stoker (13)	138
Daniel Norton (13)	139
Stacey Davidson (11)	140
Alex Bills (12)	141
Christina Bailey (13)	141
Kathryn Simm (12)	142
Louise Pearson (11)	143
Stuart Ranson (11)	143
Ellen Ridley (11)	144
Abigail Smith (12)	144
Louise Taylor (11)	145
Becci Smith (12)	146
Tabitha Dickinson (11)	147
Daniel Harrison (11)	148
Katherine Saunders (11)	148
Alex Richings (13)	149
Alison Waltham (11)	150
Sean Mullen (11)	150
Dean Stewart (11)	151
Emma McCullen (12)	151
Alex Turnbull (11)	152
Phillip McKenna (12)	152

Charlotte Maughan (12)   153
  Alison Peel (12)   153
  Jonathan Lloyd (11)   154
  Andrew McCarton (11)   155
  Alicia Forster (11)   156

Polam Hall School
  Abby Glass (13)   157
  Jade Clark (14)   157
  Jessica Crawford (13)   158
  Lucinda Bailey Thompson (14)   158
  Rebecca Harrison (13)   159
  Lucy Downes (13)   159
  Polly Enevoldson (13)   160
  Lydia Burnside-Hughes (13)   160
  Dominique Forrest (13)   161
  Hannah Dent Noble (14)   161
  Kate Sayer (13)   162
  Lucy Watson (13)   162
  Vicki Lauren Pugh (13)   163
  Emma Shakeshaft (13)   163
  Harriet Bradshaw (13)   164
  Sophie Villiers (13)   164

St Leonard's RC Comprehensive School, Durham
  Liam Wilson (14)   165
  Stephen Small (13)   165
  Emma Jackson (14)   166
  Gerard Dawson (13)   166
  Danilo Campoli (13)   166
  Anthony Davison (14)   167
  Jessica Longstaff (14)   167
  Ross Spedding (13)   167
  Sarah Tracey (14)   168
  Craig Kelly (15)   168
  Nickola Murphy (14)   169
  Sean Kelly (13)   169
  Alan Devonport (14)   170
  Thomas Bradley (13)   170
  Jess Baldasera (15)   171
  Charlotte Davies (15)   171

Christine Melvin (15)	172
Philip Morris (15)	172
James Smith (16)	173
Stephanie Hannah (15)	173
Matt Stokoe (15)	174
Ruth Innes (15)	174
Anna Craig (15)	175
Laura Armstrong (15)	175
Arthika Sripathy (15)	175
Meghan McCarthy (15)	176
Jonathan Todd (13)	176
Emma Crilley (15)	177
Laura Burnip (13)	177
Yvonne Zhang (15)	178
Stefanie Castellanos (15)	178
Amy Cooke (13)	178
Sarah Churlish (15)	179
Emma Bird (13)	179
Marissa Morgan (13)	180

Spennymoor Comprehensive School

Jessica Richardson & Natalie O'Connor	180
Rebecca McKenzie	181

The Poems

Rag Dolls

In the day,
sweet as can be.
A cute, little smile,
a pretty dress.
They sleep.

At night,
in the black,
in a creaking house,
when no one's around,
they come alive.

No longer cute,
an evil grin,
together they explore,
or wait,
for you.

Creeping in the dark,
sneaking in the cold.
Howling in the distance,
knocking at the door.
Then footsteps.

Trying to open,
the old creaking door.
More footsteps behind them,
a child's chuckle.
The break of dawn.

In the day,
sweet as can be,
a cute little smile,
a pretty dress.
They sleep.

Charlotte McAuley (13)
Carmel RC Technology College

My Hallowe'en Scare

It was a starry Hallowe'en
And all were at rest,
The moon was the only thing seen.
I was lying awake, when I heard loud footsteps
They were piercing and awfully keen.

I clambered up out of my bed,
Being careful my parents didn't wake.
My heart was racing, I felt so scared,
Making sure the silence didn't break.
Finally came the top of the stairs I'd reached.

Creak, creak, a step at a time,
That's when I met my match,
A hairy, vile monster the colour of lime
For him I was the night's first catch,
As he moved closer to me, with every climb.

Bang! Crash, Wallop! I let out a scream
The creature flew towards me in an unsettling manner.
The light shone from his eyes in a beam
'No, help,' I heard myself stammer.
That's when I woke up . . .
My Hallowe'en scare was all a dream!

Rebecca Eldrington (13)
Carmel RC Technology College

Spook

On October 31st I strolled around an eerie castle,
It was twelve o'clock, dark and scary.
Thunder rumbled while lightning flashed,
A wind howled as I ran off in a dash.
A murky mist crept over the castle
As I leapt over some rats causing hassle.
A dark figure staggered towards me in the murky gloom,
Then I thought, *this is the end, this is my doom!*

William Jones (13)
Carmel RC Technology College

The Face Of Death

Hallowe'en, trick or treat,
Look for a house you would like to meet.
Walk past the gates of glowing red,
'Go in, go in,' the persuasive voice said.
You walk in horror to the door, to its size you are inferior.
In you go feeling scared
Carry on, do you dare?
A creepy voice, the final nail
All chances to run have now failed.
Chains rattle, a scream, a shriek,
Is it a human or is it a freak?
A white figure flows down the stairs,
This ruthless burden you cannot bear.
Look around in toil and fear,
Look for the door, you try not to hear.
Look around, use your head,
Are you alive or are you dead?
It comes closer, say a prayer,
Is it here to kill or scare?
It glares at you, fangs are out,
You try to run, yell and shout.
The doors are locked in the ruthless house,
The flames of fear you try to douse.
The haunting menace is now closer,
Its tyrannic hands touch your shoulders.
A venomous pain leaks through your arms,
Now you know it means you harm.
The creature's voice evil, vexed,
Says now you're done, who will be next?

Mark Delaney (14)
Carmel RC Technology College

A Fright In The Night

As the howling wolf let out an unearthly shriek,
The graveyard arose,
The mist hung over the gravestone's peak,
The bat awoke from its little doze.

Then out of the blue an owl flew by making a deafening hoot,
What was happening to me seemed so surreal,
As the thunder clapped and the lightning did shoot,
Oh what a sense of fear I did feel.

A figure jumped out and flashed a knife,
I vowed to myself not to come here again,
I ran for the gates to escape with my life,
I finally made it to the safety of the lane.

My heart was pounding and missing a beat,
Seeing my home was a fantastic sight,
I dashed up the path and fell on the familiar seat,
My, oh my! What a terrible night!

Katie Oxley (13)
Carmel RC Technology College

Spooky Poem

On top of the wardrobe, all covered in dust,
There lives a great big spider, coloured like rust.
Shrieking and squeaking throughout the night,
Filling the household with fear and fright.
As the mice scurry around, as my heart goes pound, pound, pound.
The noise is severe, waking the household
And causing much fear.
Early in the morning just before light,
All of the noises have gone from the night.

Thomas Stokell (13)
Carmel RC Technology College

The Mouth Of Hell

The path is winding like a snake,
I've been on it so long that my legs ache.
I hear voices in the dark,
Howl and wail, do Hell's dogs bark?
I hear voices in my ear
They're confusing me so, I want to get out of here!
There are demons in front of my eyes
And they fly up to stormy skies;
Some are coming back,
One has a child whose hair is black.
The poor child, it fills me with such sorrow,
To think it won't see tomorrow.
But wait, what's this I see, a light shining,
It seems so bright to me.
A fiery furnace, dangerously hot,
Help, I like it not!

Elizabeth Sutcliffe (13)
Carmel RC Technology College

A Leaf's Autumn

Trees have blossomed colourful hair
Orange, red, yellow, but some are bare.
The leaves glide through the air
Where they land, they do not care
Leaves are scattered everywhere!

On the ground they peacefully lie
Until a footstep makes them cry.
Crunch, crackle, snap, crunch, crackle, snap.
There they are, left to wither and die,
Until next year when again they will fly.

James Potts (11)
Carmel RC Technology College

Autumn

The dew on the grass
The carpet of leaves
The dead trees ahead
None gather to bereave.

The frost bites the land
The summer has passed,
The warmth has gone
The winter is cast.

The days are all fading
The light is concealed,
The midnight is coming
The darkness revealed.

The firelight is flickering
But soon it be done,
The whistling wind,
Whispering, *autumn has come.*

Thomas Wilson (11)
Carmel RC Technology College

In The Dark

The lightning flash lit up the dark,
An owl hooted in the park,
Then thunder clapped,
Tree branches snapped,
The rusty gates ground on the floor,
A stranger knocks upon my door,
Screams echo through the night,
Screams of terror, screams of fright,
Cries for help,
Footsteps clutter,
Trip and slip,
End in the gutter!

Sophie Mackay (13)
Carmel RC Technology College

A Dream

The land of the doomed,
Nowhere to run
And the thunder has boomed.
Were you to know
What lay in your dream?
Perhaps you would've known,
What you've just seen.
That figure moves past,
But it was much too fast.
The sweat runs down
Over your frown.
You want to run
But you don't think you can.
Suddenly a hand grabs your neck
And you wake with a start,
It was just a dream.
No need to worry
But next night it's there
And there's nowhere to run!

Patrick Wharton (13)
Carmel RC Technology College

Ghost Train

It was late, it was dark,
As we walked through the park.
Then a noise from the trees,
Made me run with unease.
It was soft, but concise,
And it said very nice,
'Can you help? Can you help?'
And again, 'Can you help?'
As I stood to decide
To go or to hide.
My friend shouted, 'Clyde,
It's your turn for the ride.'

Abbi Fluen (14)
Carmel RC Technology College

Autumn Mornings

On a cold autumn morning
The frost has come without warning,
The conkers fall with a thud
Whilst I almost slip in the mud.

The morning is now dark
I tend not to go through the park,
But I just love the colours of the leaves
I asked for a new scarf, I did say please!

The animals have now gone,
They're not coming out till the sun has shone,
Everything has come without warning
I just love the autumn morning!

Becca Webber (11)
Carmel RC Technology College

The Vampire

It was the dead of night,
Something was in sight.
It was coming near,
It had no fear.

The figure was coming into shape,
It had a big long cape.
It was stood next to a grave,
But he gave nothing away.

I was getting scared,
I thought it was a vampire in his lair.
It stopped at the grave and started to stare,
He was as angry as a grizzly bear.

Rachel Musgrave (13)
Carmel RC Technology College

The Winter's Night

It's October 31st at twelve of the clock,
Such a ghostly hour,
Trees rustling, on a rain belting, winter's night
Owls hooting on a bare branch,
Panicking children creep up to the black gates.

They begin to walk down the isolated path
Jittering and shaking as their hearts pound
But never did they realise
A peculiar shadow casting from behind them.

The footsteps grew louder,
The wind became stronger,
Shutters on the windows began to clash
As there was an almighty flash of lightning.

The children bunched together
Staring at a large, old wretched house,
Pitch-black inside, nobody can hide
As they moved closer to the door
The highest ear-plucking screech was made.

The door opened,
The casting shadow pushed the children inside,
The door slammed,
There was another flash of lighting
And an almighty scream . . .

Samantha Gardiner (14)
Carmel RC Technology College

The Vampire Who Did Not Stop And Stare

There was a vampire,
Who looked like he was wearing a mask.
He said nothing, but stuck to the task.
Beware, for he did not stop and stare,
It was the graveyard which kept him there.

The deep of night was still,
Moonlight glowed on those below,
Thunder clapped
And lightning flashed,
Rain lashed down
Whilst the wind howled around.

The vampire stopped and found
The grave he had been looking for.
The grave read,
'This is the grave of Mary O'Day
Who died not knowing her right way.
Her right was clear, her will was strong,
But all along, she was not the one
Who did wrong'.

The vampire stopped and a tear fell,
He said, 'Well, we will be reunited again.'

Liam Coates (13)
Carmel RC Technology College

Autumn Time

Autumn is about the leaves on the trees,
Changing from bright green to rosy reds.
It is amazing, ambers and yawning yellows
It is then that they dance,
Swirl to the ground
And turn crispy brown.

Autumn is about shiny, dark brown conkers
Lying in the churchyard waiting to be found
Excited children on bright, cloud-free days.

Bethany Harper (11)
Carmel RC Technology College

Autumn Has Sprung

In the crisp autumn morning
While the sun is slowly dawning
The birds awake and begin to sing
While the little hedgehog feels like a king.

The sun is big and bright, high in the sky
While the birds stop singing and begin to fly,
The autumn leaves crunch under foot
And the gardener inspects the hedges for which one to cut.

Down in the allotments the food starts to die
Just like the leaves, on the ground they lie,
The geese and the swans find it cold and fly south
And the thrushes and crows have lots of food in their mouth.

The creatures and bugs get ready for hibernation
While the geese and the swans are approaching their destination.

Theo Lyonette (11)
Carmel RC Technology College

Dracula

Dracula is scary, Dracula is frightening,
His horrific eyes scare in lightning.
They're red, they're sharp, not missing a thing,
Straight face he keeps, as he is the king.

He's getting older as days go by,
But he is the soul that will never die.
He lives in a mansion that is devilishly great
He sits in his chair until very late.

His sinful teeth make room for flesh,
He likes his meal, but he likes it fresh;
Not dead, not out, but living free,
His human targets so easy to see.

Ross Kelly (13)
Carmel RC Technology College

A Dark, Dark Place

In a small, small town,
In a dark, dark place,
The wind whistled and creaked.

In the dark, dark place,
Was a big, big bang,
People scattered and fled.

In the scary, scary graveyard,
The dead, dead people,
Rose and wandered again.

But the bad, bad thing was
They really didn't know that
They were really, really dead!

The living dead had risen,
As the daytime came to a close.

In a small, small town,
In a dark, dark place,
It was never the same again!

Hannah Miller (13)
Carmel RC Technology College

Autumn Days

The trees are going bare
And everyone seems to stare.
The conkers are falling
The fog is forming.
As the leaves make a carpet on the floor
It always crunches but never to more.
People breathe like they're smoking
And for the cars they do as well.
Every time the leaves fall, the tree has no clothes,
But what about bagging someone's?

Alice Daniel (11)
Carmel RC Technology College

Hallowe'en Horror

It was twelve of the clock
Midnight had struck,
The owl hooted in the dimness
It was pitch-black.
Not a glimpse of light existed,
In an isolated, creepy place
Cries for help echoed
No one was in sight
Just a hazy fog.
The moon shone brightly
On a strange man's face,
Eyes were full of hatred
Skin was ghostly white.
Pearly, dagger-white teeth
Dripped with glistening blood,
He glided closer
And closer towards me,
Searching for his next innocent victim.

Laura Blake (13)
Carmel RC Technology College

Autumn Feeling

Remember, remember,
The month of November,
All the leaves have gone,
People squeal to make the meals.

People tuck their children into bed,
Leaves are turning crispy,
The golden carpet crunches underfoot,
As the misty mornings draw near.

The dark nights creep up,
The bare bones of the trees appear,
Bears are sleeping in their caves,
While the parents snore away.

Kirsty Coleman (13)
Carmel RC Technology College

Spooky Hallowe'en

Cold, dark, spooky Hallowe'en,
You see things that you don't want to see
Not in your nightmares, not in your dreams,
Ghostly going's on in the house next door,
Bats flying across the ebony sky,
Spiders across the floor.
Witches casting their wicked spell,
Vampires seeking their next victim,
With the sound of he graveyard bell.
Monsters under your bed,
Skeletons in your closet.
Rats swarming from the sewer they had fled
Black cats with ruby eyes
Children in their Hallowe'en costumes
Dressing in disguise.

Charlotte Lancaster (13)
Carmel RC Technology College

Autumn Has Arrived

Autumn time has now arrived
The misty clouds and dense fog thrive,
The flames of fires twist and turn
As the logs and branches slowly burn,
Autumn time has come.
The gale-force winds blow at the trees
As the leaves fall slowly in the breeze,
As they fall the trees look thinner
Out of sun and rain, the rain's the winner
Autumn time has come.
As people gradually disappear
In the whistling wind which you can hear,
As the foliage falls to the ground
People are in their homes, safe and sound.

Paul McDermott (11)
Carmel RC Technology College

The Night Monster

As I walked from the misty graveyard,
There was a voice I heard.
Creatures creating a spine-chilling plan,
As I gazed around and observed.

The rustling of leaves, the rattle of the gates,
It was getting scary now.
Then a laugh, a haunting laugh,
It could not be a monster, how?

I heard footsteps getting closer and closer,
Whispers came from behind the trees.
Suddenly, a black figure loomed over,
I couldn't move, I was in a freeze.

It moved closer, its hot breath smothered my face,
It spoke once and bit - that was the end of me.

So that was the story of Hallowe'en
That shows creatures hide in the night.
So when you're in a graveyard at night,
Don't stop, because it could be the end of you that night!

Thomas Haile (13)
Carmel RC Technology College

Autumn Poem

The leaves are fluttering to the ground,
The trees are losing their hair.

The mornings are getting darker and soggier,
The dew is like a sheet of water over the grass.

The flames dance joyfully in the fire,
People putting in logs to keep themselves warm.

Animals find food for the winter
Hiding in their burrows, getting ready to hibernate.

Out of sight, conkers spend whole summers
Growing spiky in a leafy corner.

Neil Hanlon (11)
Carmel RC Technology College

Characteristics Of Autumn

Look at the frost,
So crisp, so clean,
Like frosted diamond,
Sprinkled over the cold, hard ground.

The leaves are swirling and twirling,
Twisting and turning
And finally landing,
With a satisfying crunch.

The conkers descend,
Dropping like bombs,
Landing with a crack,
As with a bang they explode.

The first flakes of snow are falling,
Like frozen winter stars,
The leaves are gone, the nights are black
And autumn's gone afar.

Natasha Redpath (12)
Carmel RC Technology College

Autumn Is Coming

Autumn is here, the leaves have fallen
Into a patchwork blanket,
The trees are bare bones
You can hear them whispering.
They reach out to grab you
With their hard hands,
People by the fire watching it dance
Turning red, yellow and orange.
The morning is dark and gloomy
No one is out, they're alone,
Twirling, you don't hear a crunch
Not a sound, only the autumn coming
Coming, coming for us.

Louise Sowerby (11)
Carmel RC Technology College

Crunch, Crunch

Conkers falling from the trees
Along with all the leaves
Yellow, brown and orange too
Parents know what to do.
Get the coal on the fire
Fire roaring like a lion,
The wind howls like a dog
Look outside and see the fog.
Drip, drop, drip, drop, goes the rain
Driving the parents insane,
The trees look like they are in pain
The leaves blowing all around
Making a crunchy sound.
The lovely coloured leaves
Will soon be covered in snow.

Kay Hardisty (12)
Carmel RC Technology College

Autumn Life

As the wind shrieks and wails,
When the sky begins to hail.
The leaves somersault in the air,
As the wind blows through our hair.

As the leaves cover the ground
Children run round and round.
The children play and run,
People screaming and having fun.

The dew on the grass
Each morning I pass.
The fires roar
As life is no longer a bore.

Laura Myers (12)
Carmel RC Technology College

Autumn Wonders

Happily, gracefully the leaves fall to the ground,
At the bottom of the tree a great big mound.
All of the trees, they look so bare,
Because they've got no leaves to wear.

The dancing flames in the open fire,
In time to the Christmas choir,
Rehearsing for the near time,
When all those presents will soon be mine.

But we're still in the season before,
In which happens a lot, lot more.
All Hallows Eve and Bonfire Night,
Fireworks shooting into the sky with all their might!

Andrew Jordan (12)
Carmel RC Technology College

Autumn Feelings

The crunch of the crispy leaves under my feet,
The feeling of a hedgehog's prickles on my hand,
The smell of a bonfire as it reaches my nose.

The golden leaves twirl to the ground,
The brown hedgehog scuttles away,
The orange fire dies down.

The morning comes, light breaks free,
And the little brown hedgehog's looking at me.

The darkness comes, light fades away
And the little brown hedgehog's here to stay.

Sophie Norman (11)
Carmel RC Technology College

The Autumn Weeks

As the cold autumn starts,
The birds start to part
The nights get longer,
The winds get stronger.

The leaves start to fall,
The children have a ball
Playing with the conkers
It's as if they've gone bonkers.

The leaves are yellow, brown and red,
Crumbling on the floor when dead,
Farmers harvest their crops,
Hard, brown acorns begin to drop.

Some people stay in bed,
Some go outside and turn rosy red,
The weather gets colder,
The winds get bolder and bolder.

The leaves swirl to the ground,
Making no sound,
The floor, a carpet of colour,
The trees not as full.

The weather gets worse,
People start to curse,
Winter starts to creep up,
The temperature doesn't seem to come up.

Hannah Gohr (12)
Carmel RC Technology College

Autumn Days

Autumn days are coming near
All the squirrels full of fear,
A pavement full of browns and reds
As the children lay in their beds.

The leaves from the trees sway to the floor
Trying to block the door,
A foggy, misty, damp day
As the brown and red leaves blow away.

Children are ready, time to play
Playing conkers on a rainy day,
The leaves are all soggy
The days are all foggy.

The flames of the fire and dancing,
Outside the children and toddlers are prancing.
The leaves are crunching,
The squirrels are munching.

The birds are tweeting
As they are eating.
Al the squirrels full of fear
As autumn days are drawing near.

Melissa Sample (12)
Carmel RC Technology College

The Glorious Season

The multicoloured leaves fall to the sodden ground
The dazzling carpet of colours lay on the floor.
Hats, gloves and scarves children wear,
The cold air blows making a sweet, whistling sound.

Murky fog in the midnight, black sky
The trees stripped bare to their bones,
Children smoking without cigarettes,
Animals hibernate, the world is stripped bare.

Robyn Ward (11)
Carmel RC Technology College

Autumn Poem

On a bitterly cold morning
The old, lonesome tree is creaking, moaning
Waiting for his time to come . . .

As the wind whistles over the moors,
The withered tree shudders
And a curtain of cascading leaves descend,
Tumbling, twisting and gliding in the breeze.

While the bonfires crackle and dance,
Licking the wood they stand upon
The tree lives on,
Its bones now bare . . .

The rain begins to hammer down
The murky fog now closes in,
Animals scurrying to construct their homes,
Ready to hibernate at this time of year.

Weak and groaning,
The wounded tree's feet begin to crack and split
With a final creak the roots break free
And the forgotten soldier collapses in the twilight.

Lorna Goldsmith (12)
Carmel RC Technology College

Autumn Days

Midnight black nights are approaching us now,
The wind is whistling and the fog is misty,
The trees are beginning to get crinkled skin
And the leaves are turning rich, red colours.

Animals prepare their homes for winter,
While we stack up the logs in the fire,
The flames dance with happiness,
The leaves twirl and swirl to the ground,
Like the trees getting rid of their friends.

Rebecca King (11)
Carmel RC Technology College

Autumn

The time is autumn
Winter's begun,
Conkers everywhere,
Children having fun.
It is soon time for the bonfire night.

As people stare
The trees become bare,
The trees rustle
The conkers fall,
People with bags clean them up.
They soon go home.

Leaves rustle loudly
The path
Is no longer a path,
It becomes a carpet of leaves.
The bonfires burn
They soon die down.
Autumn has just begun.

Adam Davison (12)
Carmel RC Technology College

Year 10

This is me in Year 10,
All this course work is doing my head in,
Deadlines and dates, that's all you hear these days,
Better get it finished, can't be late,
Talking about stress in PHSE
Well that's what I have got, they all tell me,
Ah well, another 18 months to go,
Then that's it, that's all I have to know.

Victoria Mackenzie (14)
Carmel RC Technology College

Darkness Of The Night

Out in the dark,
at twelve of the clock.
The trees were rustling
and the wind was whistling.
Wolves howling.
owls hooting.
In the loneliness of the night,
footsteps came in the background.
Closer and closer it was getting,
louder and louder the heartbeat was going.
Lightning struck,
thunder clapped,
as the moon came out of the darkness
it was as calm as the breeze.

Alisha Sinha (13)
Carmel RC Technology College

The Carpet Of Leaves

As I walk along the carpet of leaves,
I see red, orange and green,
I hear crunch, crackle and rustle,
As I walk along the carpet of leaves,
I see leaves as bright as a fire,
I hear children's gleeful laughter,
As I walk along the carpet of leaves,
I see leaves swirling, swaying and swooping,
I hear the strong wind, blowing the leaves around,
As I walk along the carpet of leaves,
I see a bonfire roaring like a lion,
I hear the birds chirping,
As I walk along the carpet of leaves,
This is what greets me.

Nicola Bleasby (12)
Carmel RC Technology College

Autumn Days

Leaves fall down
Leaving the trees extremely bare,
Walking down the path
You need to take care.

The days go by
Getting colder and colder
And autumn goes by
Getting older and older.

Conkers, chestnuts and leaves
Are the things on the floor,
I can hear the rustling
Through my door.

The dark nights are coming closer
Winter's drawing in,
Jack Frost stands there
With a large grin.

Darren Swankie (13)
Carmel RC Technology College

Autumn's Sensation

Children playing under chestnut trees,
Skipping in the autumn breeze.
Red, orange, yellow and green,
All of the glorious colours to be seen.
During autumn's wonderful creation,
Animals settle into hibernation.
Leaves of orange, gold and red
Geese are flying overhead.
Going south for their migration
During this wonderful autumn sensation.

Christina Muller (13)
Carmel RC Technology College

Oh Autumn, Oh Autumn

Oh autumn, oh autumn
The beautiful, colourful season.
If you're not fond of autumn
You can't have a good reason.

With the smell of smoke
From the sizzling bonfire light,
And a Hallowe'en party scare
In a room as dark as night.

Oh autumn, oh autumn,
With sounds of every season.
The lovely dance of bitter leaves,
Falling for some sad reason.

The weather's awfully freezing
Condensation on all glass.
The dew and fog take control
Like the frost already has.

Oh autumn, oh autumn,
The smells of every season.
The apples and pears fall to the floor
Which, itself is freezing.

The cute and cold squirrels squeak
And each of them plays along,
But soon they'll start hibernation
So they can stay strong.

Oh autumn, oh autumn,
The beautiful, colourful season.
You must be fond of autumn,
As now there's no good reason.

Michael Thurloway (12)
Carmel RC Technology College

Autumn's Beauty

Autumn, people often say
Is the worst season of them all,
But as I look at the world today
I just want to shout and bawl,
'Have you seen al these beautiful things
Or are you blind to life?'
Because I do not think these things
Are going to hurt you or your wife.

With the crunch of leaves
And the splash of puddles,
The old, bare trees
All colours in a middle.
There are greens and browns
And yellows and oranges,
Kids in the towns
And families with porridges.

Bonfires that roar
And animals hiding
Wood choppers saw
And the little kids are riding.
Now and then rain starts to pour
But it always keeps withdrawing.

Richard McAllister (12)
Carmel RC Technology College

Night Wish

I look into your eyes and see a view that's ocean deep.
Look into your mind and see a story of a love you tried to keep.

Then I touch your skin, it's as frosty as a phantom.
In your heart a river with nothing at the bottom.

This dream I do believe is the opposite of bliss.
I am sorry my friend, you are not my night wish.

Rachael Peeke (14)
Carmel RC Technology College

Autumn

Mornings are foggy and misty,
The dark nights approach,
The sun goes down quicker
And there is less light.
Light becomes dark in most of England,
Fires get lit, oranges and reds mix.

Crackling flames dance,
Trees are bare with no leaves,
Leaves are swirling
Down onto the golden floor.

The wind howls
It whistles through the trees.
The leaves fall and flutter
And dance around my feet.

As the rain comes down
The places begin to flood,
Trees and crops get destroyed
In the terrible flood waters.

Sam Jinks (11)
Carmel RC Technology College

Autumn's Creation

Look at the kids playing with conkers,
    They must be all going bonkers.
Look at the parents sat inside,
    I think they must be trying to hide.
Look at the animals in hibernation,
    Look at God's wonderful creation.
Think of the amazing things around us,
    How they give me such a buzz.
Now this poem has come to an end,
    I think I've driven you round the bend.

Christopher Ward (12)
Carmel RC Technology College

Autumn's Arrived

Crackle, crunch go the leaves
As they fall from the trees,
They decorate the path
Leaving a carpet of colour.

The whistling wind howls
In the black, foggy night,
The hissing rain goes splash on the grass,
Making it soaky and damp.
The mad mist blinds people on their way.

Families sit in the warm
The coal sizzling and crackling in the background
No shivers to be seen, just happiness
Reloading the coal, as they await the night.

Burning their food
The animals prepare,
Messing up lawns and rushing crazily.

Autumn has now arrived.

Leah Kennedy (11)
Carmel RC Technology College

The Magic Of Autumn

The leaves start to crisp, crunch and change
The weather dulls and frost starts to appear,
The blazing fire roars like a growling lion
And the howling wind shrieks through the trees.
Children start jumping on carpets of leaves,
Squirrels go hunting for acorns and chestnuts,
Leaves flutter down like a multicoloured butterfly.
Then the midnight sky starts to spread across the town
And beaming fireworks glitter in the sky.
People go inside as the nights get longer,
To snuggle in front of the crackling fire.

Jade Towse (13)
Carmel RC Technology College

Autumn Days

There is a puddle, I keep going in a muddle,
All day there are no kids to play.
Red, orange, yellow and brown,
I look through my window glaring with a frown.
The rain has stopped, we all come out,
Get together and mess about.
Jumping and smashing, there's wind about
Dress warmly so we don't get knocked out.
We zip up our jackets to keep us warm,
Have a huge stretch and then a yawn.
Sprint to the finish jump for a mile,
Take a huge leap and land in a pile.
Stick up your arm and shout hooray,
Enjoy the rest of your autumn day!

Robert Corless (12)
Carmel RC Technology College

Dracula's Territory

Do not set foot upon this land
As this is where the vampire stands,
Even standing near the gate
Will almost definitely seal your fate.
If you see him in his gown
Make a mad dash down to the town,
If he starts to pursue you
Just make sure you know what to do.
If you are a cop with a gun
Please just try to shoot and run,
Run very fast, don't let him ahead
Just dash for your life, get to your bed.
But if you have two feet of lead,
That will simply make you dead.

Kieren Kemp (13)
Carmel RC Technology College

Me And You

If you think it's all right to talk about me,
You are wrong beyond belief.
To say all those things and lie to me
And cause me oh so much grief.

How can you smile at me and expect
Me to be smiling back at you.
The deceit in your eyes affects
The way I now look at you.

You tell your side of the story,
The side that we both know ain't true.
I know that you are about to lie,
You are impeccably right on cue.

I really thought I could trust you,
This much I know is true.
You never used to be like this,
What happened to you?

Kyrie Hunter (14)
Carmel RC Technology College

Autumn Poem

The fire flickers with light,
The moon shines so bright.
The bare trees sway,
As the children play.

People wailing
The rain hailing.
Birds hiding,
Leaves flying.

The leaves dashing,
The fire flashing.
The sun goes way,
The children stay in and play.

Sadie McCartney (12)
Carmel RC Technology College

Christmas

Christmas is a time of joy,
A little boy plays with his toy,
He only got one this year,
His dad lost his job because of beer.
His mummy left them by themselves
So no delivery from Christmas elves.

Christmas is a time of joy,
A woman has a new baby boy,
He snores and gurgles all night
All wrapped up in blankets of white.
Happy tears roll out of her eyes
They hold no secrets, no anger, no lies.

Christmas is a time of joy
Maybe not for every girl and boy,
Behind every concealed door
Are people who are rich and poor.
Not everyone leads happy lives
Some people's lives are full of knives.

Kate Barker (15)
Carmel RC Technology College

When Satan Comes

When Satan comes to Earth
There will be nothing we can do.

He will turn our Earth into a fiery jail
Our race will surely fail.

When he unleashes his demons
To roam throughout the land,
No one will be left to stand.

He will burn the grass and trees
And turn the rivers into the blood of his victims.

Thomas Ward (13)
Carmel RC Technology College

Autumn's Creation

Kicking and demolishing leaf piles
All the children have huge smiles.
Red, orange, yellow and green
Are all the colours to be seen.
The wind is gushing and whirling,
Sending all the leaves twirling.
All the dark and creepy nights
Give all the family the frights.
Now autumn's halfway through,
Stupid trick or treaters come to my door and say, *Boo!*
Because now it's autumn's wonderful creation,
Animals go into hibernation.
And this poem is such a sensation
Well, I'm not sure about that anyway.

Steven Brack (12)
Carmel RC Technology College

An Autumn Day

The wind howls in the east,
The sun sets in the west.
The crackle of the fire burning brightly,
Kids playing with their conkers,
The fog lies ahead like a dark cloud hovering above.

The nights get colder,
The days get shorter,
The leaves crunch like cornflakes.

The acorns fall, crops turn gold,
The cold autumn day is coming,
So watch out for the sights.

Paul Jefferson (12)
Carmel RC Technology College

Autumn

I love autumn,
From the colour of the leaves,
To the chill of the wind.
Sitting by the fire I like to dream.
What would it be like,
To have a year full of autumn?
We could watch the fireworks zooming
Across the sky at night,
The trick or treaters
Scare and fright.
This would all be very well,
But having a year full of autumn,
I could never tell,
What would it be like to have a year full of heat?
Where the sun shone bright
And we paddled our feet.
I think that a year
Of winter would be best,
With snow laid lightly upon the floor,
And oh yes, you know the score,
Santa Claus we would see soar!

Bethany Heard (15)
Carmel RC Technology College

School

I've got to get some information
To get an education,
But I'm in desperation
Because of my discrimination.
To books with information,
Instead I watch Coronation
Street or play on my PlayStation.
I need a vacation!
To ease my frustration.

Chris Kelly (14)
Carmel RC Technology College

Scared To Die

It was dark, unearthly and a misty old night,
The owls and the rats lurking about.
There was a strange feel to the eerie atmosphere,
And suddenly before I knew it, this mask of death drew closer
                                                        and closer.
I was scared, horrified and not prepared to die,
But I could feel the satanic ghost come closer by.
I scrutinised around, no exit in sight,
I panicked and fell to the rock-like path.
Seconds had passed; I was awakened by a light,
A boisterous voice then lay upon me.
I could feel my body collapsing inside,
My death was nearing each minute that went by,
But soon I awakened in my humble home,
Lazing in my bed, I wondered confusingly - was this a reality or a lie?
I am left with a scar of my terrifying ordeal
And the memories that lurk in the deadly yard.

Sophie Daniel (14)
Carmel RC Technology College

Evil

It was twelve of the clock,
It was an eerie, corrupt place to live.
Wolves howling, owls hooting,
There were voices in the air.
No one will survive,
There were loud bangs, thuds and crashes,
Shocking noises coming from the bushes.
There were loud noises, more terrifying than ever.
I felt scared, exhausted, this was a terrible place,
There were screams in the air
As I waited, along the dark, gloomy streets.

James Dixon (13)
Carmel RC Technology College

Skiing On The Snow

On the coach and off we go,
All anxious to get on the snow.
A few hours had gone, but it seemed like forever,
We arrived at Dover and got on the ferry together.
Over the sea, waving and bumping,
Everyone's stomach turning and thumping.
Back on the coach, with many hours ahead
Everyone wishing they were at home in bed.
Then Miss called out, 'Only 26 hours to go!'
'Oh when, oh when will we be on the snow?'
The day passed by we had slept through the night
Waking up to see the sun shining bright.
We were in Italy, the resort only two hours away,
Everyone looking forward to our stay.
We got to the hotel, everyone ready to go
Tomorrow, tomorrow, we will be on the snow!

Sarah McDonogh (14)
Carmel RC Technology College

The Golden Season

Its days so cold and muddy
The bellowing wind and creeping fog
With the heavy rain and thick clouds
Blocking the sun from shining its perpetual light.

Trees of every kind wither
And their leaves sweep and swoop
And float to the ground
Scattering in every direction
Amongst the conkers.

Its colours are appearing all around
Orange, brown, yellow and gold
Like a multicoloured carpet swaying vigorously
Animals flee to their homes to hibernate
And nature goes to sleep.

Calum Fovargue (12)
Carmel RC Technology College

Rugby, That Gentleman's Game

Two teams strive for victory
In the tunnel they meet,
In battle they will collide.
Laden with armour,
Scrum caps as helmets,
Shoulder pads for breast plates.
The whistle is the war cry
Forwards, forward,
Backs behind,
Wings to the side,
Muscle hits muscle,
Skill against skill.
Ball goes out, line-outs thrown,
Balls kicked, through the posts,
Is it won?
Celebration for the victors,
Smiles from the vanquished,
Three cheers for all,
Applause all around!

Adam Sadler (14)
Carmel RC Technology College

Autumn Is Here

Swirling, whirling,
Autumn is here,
Frosty, icy rain shatters,
Red, orange and green.
All the colours of the leaves,
From different types of trees.

Animals hibernate,
Whilst children skate,
On the massive ice rink,
Nearly all day.

Amy Raper (11)
Carmel RC Technology College

Hip Hop Rhymes

Razel the godfather of noise
He's hanging wid all da boys,
Eminem and Dr Dre too
The crowds noise is *wo, oo, oo.*
Razel drops da beats
Eminem with the vocal feats,
Dre is on the stage
Reading those rhymes right off the page.
Then turns up the D O double G,
It's Snoop Doggy Dog for the 2003.
He's ridin' down the empty street
Everyone runs to him just to meet.
This pimp daddy rulz the roost
It gives the crowd a big huge boost.
The music stops, it all goes quiet
The large crowd nearly causes a riot.
The show's all over now,
The lyrical masterminds all take a bow.

Daniel Fox (15)
Carmel RC Technology College

Poems Are Hard To Write

Poems are hard to write,
They all give me a fright,
Words never come to age
Across my page,
Poems are hard to write.

Poems are hard to write,
I try with all my might,
I have no inspiration
In this moment of desperation,
Poems are hard to write.

Jack Ridley (14)
Carmel RC Technology College

Untitled

It was a dusky, foreboding, frightful night,
All he could feel was fright.
The threatening thunder sounds, scaring him deadly.
Nowhere to run, nowhere to go,
But the rain kept lashing down.
He saw a figure in the distance,
Still nowhere to run, nowhere to go.
The figure advanced, the man gave him a fright,
Sent him in a trance.
He moved closer to this figure.

Still nowhere to run, nowhere to go,
He ran to a little house in the wood.
Through the dark mist and thick black mud,
He got to the door and knocked on it,
Then a figure appeared opening the door . . .
Nowhere to run, nowhere to go.

Michael Ringwood (13)
Carmel RC Technology College

Amazon

Rushing, crashing through the green,
So big and powerful like a queen,
Swinging, flowing so far away,
I'd like to see it one summer's day.

So silent yet loud,
Mysterious like a cloud,
I am the Amazon!

Rushing, crashing through the brown
Like a queen who wears a crown,
Surrounded by forest,
Look really hard and you'll find the tallest.

So silent yet loud,
Mysterious like a cloud, I am the Amazon,
Queen of the forest.

Sam Robinson (14)
Carmel RC Technology College

Christmas

'Christmas is coming,' said my mummy,
She said, 'Santa is as busy as a bumblebee.'
Next to the living room window, stands a tree
And when the lights are on it is a pretty sight to see.
Under the tree are lots of presents,
For Mum, Dad, me and baby Jessie.
Santa is dressed in white and red,
Dad says he is jolly because the wine goes to his head.
On Christmas Eve I can hardly sleep,
Knowing I won't get any presents
If I open my eyes and have a peep.
When I wake up on Christmas Day,
I scream and shout for joy,
Knowing I can play with my new toy.
I hope Santa comes early next year
And that I get a puppy with soft brown fur.

Clare Charman (14)
Carmel RC Technology College

Autumn

The swirling leaves float down gently
And the midnight black takes over the sky.

The crackling fire in the distance,
The grey fog appearing in the darkness.

The animals start to hibernate
And the squirrels quickly gather up their nuts.

All the bright colours lay on the floor,
The crackling noise of the leaves.

The branches on the trees are like bones
And the leaves are like clothes

As the dark, gloomy days get worse.

Rachel Baines (11)
Carmel RC Technology College

Autumn Begins

The children splash, splash, splash around in the pool.
Their mums and dads sit trying to keep cool.
Everyone is having a good time,
Trying to survive under the sun's blazing eye.
Not a cloud in the sky is what they look up to see.
All waiting for the refreshments at half-past three.
People keep coming endlessly through the open door.
But suddenly, a leaf falls and hits the floor.
It twists and turns like a plane but nobody can stop it hit.
They know what is happening, like last year when it repeatedly did.
No more summer swimming, relaxing or having a laugh.
It will be dark nights now onwards, having an early bath.
Autumn is on its way, hurry and wrap up tight.
The wind will try its hardest but fight it with all your might!
We'll see no more animals, they'll be underground warm.
We'll soon be seeing farmers outside scattering their corn.
At least we had a good time when summer was here.
Now we'll have to live through autumn and wait till next year.

Jonathan Way (14)
Carmel RC Technology College

Game Of Golf

Golf can be played everywhere,
When you hit that ball and it flies in the air,
You stand on the green,
Feel anxious and keen.
Grabbing your putter,
Hitting the ball like a knife slicing through butter.
The ball dropping in the circular hole,
You grab the number eighteen flag pole.
Feeling happy and glad but still alone,
You make your way back home.

Christopher Clinton (15)
Carmel RC Technology College

Who Knows What Might Lurk Beyond That Corridor?

The howling of the dog roared throughout,
Footsteps created a booming noise which echoed around and around,
The cackling of the witch herself came from behind that door,
Who knows what might lurk beyond that corridor?
The lashing of the rain made me shudder and scream,
The demonic, dark magic sorcerer yelled with all his might,
Chains clinked and clanked from under the floor,
Who knows what might lurk beyond that corridor?
A glowing light scared me so, as the candle glowed,
The owl swooped down and sat on the sill to wait for the golden ball,
The banging and crying from every brick wall
                            made me want to go on no more,
Who knows what might lurk beyond that corridor?
The clap of thunder was a sign of disaster
                as the thrash of lightning came a second after,
A cat ran past which was a sign of bad luck,
A bellowing scream gave me a sign that I couldn't go on anymore,
Who knows what might lurk beyond that corridor?

Emma Bantleman (13)
Carmel RC Technology College

Autumn

You know autumn is coming round
When all the leaves fall to the ground.
The trees move to and fro with the wind
That makes your cheeks glow.
The nights creep in and the days are short,
It's time for hats and gloves to be bought.
You hear the crunch as your feet touch the ground
As the leaves are dancing all around.
I don't feel you need anymore reasons
To explain autumn as one of the best seasons.

Kelly Bravey (14)
Carmel RC Technology College

The Room

In the dark and lonely school
a small boy, no more than twelve
walked the long, grim corridor.
Turned to an old oak door,
the breathing of the boy was heard all about.

A hoot from an owl echoed throughout,
a warning, a sign of some devious kind,
but still the boy went and opened the great door.
A moan and a groan, a grind from a door.
Still, the boy advanced
swallowed by the dark
but out came a torch from his pack.

The beam shone on cobwebs and brooms
and everything seemed fine but then . . .
out from the dark two grizzly red eyes shone
and a thud from behind his head.

Twelve of the clock, witching hour but worse . . .
ghosts and ghouls and a tricky im came,
from a cupboard a hairy, fat beast and a savage werewolf
blood dripping from a vampire's fangs.
A slimy hand touched his shoulder
and he shot ten foot in the air.

When he hit the floor he turned around,
a creature of a terrible kind.
The fangs, the nails, its breath with all the diseases inside,
the boy screamed and wailed
he dropped his torch and fled away.

So a message to all you inquisitive minds;
When the twelve of midnight arrives,
lock your doors and bar your windows
because it's Satan's slaves' playtime.
So a hoot from an owl is a warning,
a sign of a devious kind.

Chris Richardson (13)
Carmel RC Technology College

Doors

It was pitch-black on Hallowe'en night,
When we got the most fearful fright.
We knocked on a door that was rather tall,
This sinful, devilish man appeared,
We were all silent in fear.
We looked around all in tears.
Is this the end or isn't it?
We carried on a little further until another door,
The man walked off and left us alone.
We found to our horror another door.

Inside a creature on the floor
He squealed, wriggled and cried some more
The man came back to our dismay
The creature let out a howl,
The man just subdued its piercing scream.
In fear and toil we fled the house,
To hear the languish of a final scream.

Lauren Morgan (14)
Carmel RC Technology College

Autumn

Fires blazing in nice, warm homes
Roaring fires like proud, angry lions,
Leaves swaying from the trees,
Crunching leaves you can hear.
The floor is wet and boggy
The damp and soggy floor,
Children chilly and complaining,
Cold children are crying.
Sleeping animals are really very tired
In the cold, dark outdoors,
While humans snuggle up
Snuggle up in their lovely warm homes.
On dark and gloomy nights
Autumn is finally here.

Stephanie Metcalfe (12)
Carmel RC Technology College

Blood Stalker

Avoid the clownish mortals for they will seek,
Nothing but blood will they leak.
When the clock turns ten
I'll be looking for them.
Will they be frightened, will they be scared?
For they might see me, then they will be condemned.

There in the darkness they will stay,
For I am coming, then they will pray.
Blood may be spilt but not of mine,
They will try to avoid me but they won't be fine.
Pace their walk and they will slowly die,
Rush their walk and they will rapidly die.

Garlic will kill me for my despair,
Crucifix also then I'll fly to my lair.
Defeat me if they dare
For I am immortal until I can bare.
But wait, who are they, I just don't know how,
There they are, I can see them right now.

Come to me, I will make you my slaves
No wait, they can chase me to my caves.
Right I am here, I can't wait for their blood,
Should someone else drink their blood,
Or maybe I should.
Finally they are here,
Yes they have seen me,
Now it is time for them to fear me.

Dean Goldsborough (13)
Carmel RC Technology College

Autumn's Here Again

A crunchy, firey carpet lay on the path.
Trees bare and nothing to spare,
As their skin has already gone.
Autumn's here again.

Leaves red, orange and brown.
An ear-shattering wind
Frosty mornings and frosty windows.
Autumn's here again.

Coal fires roaring like tigers.
Smouldering, spitting and bright.
Warm homes and dark nights.
Autumn's here again.

Prickly conkers, their shells opening
A pathway of piercing shells.
The conkers left bare.
Autumn's here again.

Hallowe'en's here, costumes everywhere.
Pumpkin lanterns alight.
Sweets galore, something sweet to adore.
Autumn's here again.

Snow, winds blowing to and fro
Coldness is in the air,
Snow lays like icing on a cake.
Autumn's been and now it's gone.

Emma Spraggon (12)
Carmel RC Technology College

The Castle

The wind was howling,
It was pitch-black
Apart from the odd light.
No one was home in the castle,
I'm all alone
On this dark and eerie night,

With shadows casting over me,
I saw a shadow wander past me,
An owl hooted.
The clock struck twelve
As I looked up
At the big clock face tower.

The clock chimed eleven times,
But the twelfth chime was silenced,
By a blood-curdling scream.
On the top of the tower a flowing white figure,
Holding something to her breast.

Her fangs shone in the moonlight,
Like a razor-sharp knife.
She dropped the bundle from the top of the tower,
It landed with a thud.

Sinead Wisker (13)
Carmel RC Technology College

Scream!

The hood is as black as night,
It hides a murderer's head,
He knows that he can't take it off,
Or he will definitely end up dead.

He puts on his flowing, pitch-black cloak,
It hides him in the dead of night,
He hides among the shadows,
Out of people's sight.

The howling of the trees as the wind blows,
The hooting of the owls, sends a shiver down your spine,
The rattling of the chains on the graveyard gates,
He is lurking somewhere in the darkness.

The rats scurry across the gravel path,
Footsteps can be heard,
His footsteps,
Rays of moonlight shine through the mass of clouds.

The tombstones stand in the middle of the waving blades of grass,
You look closely into the forest and you can see his pure white mask,
The clock strikes twelve,
As you look back into the forest, you can no longer see . . .
Scream!

Stacey Clegg (14)
Carmel RC Technology College

Shadow

Tick-tock,
Tick-tock,
Twelve o'clock, midnight,
It's marching its way toward me,
Swoosh, flash, speed,
What could it be?
I followed it,
Lead me to the creepy mansion.
Red door looming above me,
Do I dare to enter or be chicken?
RRRR! As the door opened
A thick black shadow went up the stairs,
Should I follow it?
I stepped . . . *RRRR!* The door closed,
Left, right.
Up the stairs
Crimson blood oozing down the door handle,
Door opened, squeaking.
I saw an enormous cupboard,
Light bulb popped,
I was scared.
Child was crying,
I opened the cupboard,
Chain tangle around the child,
Unlocked chain, door closed,
Lights turned off,
I'm like a mouse.

Troy McCaskill (14)
Carmel RC Technology College

Ghostly Graveyard

I entered the graveyard at the dead of night
Nothing there but an awful sight.

I looked around, nothing there
Except for a bat with a terrifying stare.

I walked closer to this bat
But all I could see was a fearsome black cat.

I shuffled to the creaking gate,
Where you know for sure you're sealing your fate.

I came closer to this house,
But the first thing I saw was a dead mouse.

I creaking along the floorboards,
I heard a howling noise,
I looked to my left and looked to my right,
Then the bat flew in and gave me a nasty bite.

David O'Neill (13)
Carmel RC Technology College

Crazy Jewellery

If I was wearing an earring made out of slugs
Everybody would run away from me
And wouldn't be my friend.

If I was wearing a necklace made out of nuts and bolts,
My mum would say, 'Where did you get that from?'

If I was wearing rings made out of beetles,
No boys would hold my hand.

If I was wearing a bracelet made out of conkers on string,
My dad would say, 'Are you crazy?'

I'm glad I don't wear crazy jewellery!

Fay Austin (11)
Haughton Community School

My Window

It's the sun shining coldly on a winter morning,
The garage roof and puddles of water,
The birds calling,
The clanging of the factory,
People walking dogs.
Trees swaying in the wind,
It's cold and windy.
Before we go to school,
The wet, cold grass,
The rough tree trunk,
My dog enjoying the presence of others.
I can't see it but I can hear it,
It's the black, deadly crow.
It's starting to rain,
I have to go soon.
I don't want to.
This feeling is wonderful.
Why is it so beautiful?
It's Mother Nature's ways.
It's Mother Nature's ways.
My radiator is lovely and warm standing here.
I wish my life could be this wonderful,
As beautiful as this view.

Ehlana Foley (12)
Haughton Community School

Torch

It is used by children,
Adults too,
But mostly in caves
And underground lairs,
I will give you light
When there is none left.

Jayne Blackburn (11)
Haughton Community School

My Window View

Snow-topped houses.
Mud where flowers used to be,
Trees swaying in the breeze,
People laughing,
Trees swaying,
Birds flying,
People walking past,
Starting to snow,
Morning in December.
The snow is soft but freezing cold,
Footprints in the snow of a bird,
A cat purring, coming from behind the shed.
The cat will dart out from behind the shed
Because someone has just walked past.

Happy, very cold and peaceful.
Whose cat is that?
It is Ellen's cat, who lives in number 38.
It is Ellen's cat, who lives in number 38.
The telly blaring out pop music loudly.
I wish it would get warm soon.

Eve Richardson (12)
Haughton Community School

I Can't Remember

I can't remember who stole my pencil.
I can't remember whatever happened to my utensil.
I can't remember why I am stupid.
I can't remember, where is Cupid?
I can't remember when I bought a game.
I can't remember whether I was a pain.
I can't remember how I broke my wrist.
I can't remember if I even broke my wrist.

Shaun MacKenzie (11)
Haughton Community School

What A Beautiful Day

Rain taps down the window,
Leaves are falling down,
People walking past with a frown.
Birds are tucked away, lying in their nests.
Dogs sit inside bored, eating and depressed.
Cat runs under car, buses passing by,
Children coming out of school
Teachers wave goodbye.

Dad's arrived home late,
Kids are running about.
Going to McDonald's
Because the sun's come out.
Everybody's happy,
Everybody out,
But as time passes by
Bedtime is about.

Sofia Rustico (13)
Haughton Community School

Georgina Lloyd

G is for gorgeous, a loving sweetheart,
E is for energetic, talented and smart,
O is for optimistic, worthy of praise,
R is for radiant, you simply amaze!
G is for gem, so precious and true
I is for intelligent, happy to know you
N is for natural, the joy you bestow
A is for able, always on the go.

L is for likeable, top of the class
L is for loud, you're a really good lass
O is for outstanding, peaceful and kind
Y is for youthful, sound of mind
D is for different, that's me!

Georgina Lloyd (13)
Haughton Community School

My Perfect View

Factories in the distance,
Next door's garden filled with flowers.
Trickling of my neighbour's pond,
Bustling of cars on the nearby street.
Trees swaying in the breeze,
Children running on the fields.
The sun's rays shine,
And the cool wind causes a draft through my window.
A warm summer's day in the middle of July.
Soft, fluffy clouds, cold, hard concrete.
The dog in the next garden lying down,
The birds flying high in the sky.
The presence of the warm air lingers
In a while the family over the way will be back.
Calm and content as I peer out my window.
Which river's that?
The twisting River Skerne of course.
The twisting River Skerne of course.
My boring room,
How I wish I lived out there!

Lisa McCormick (12)
Haughton Community School

My Daft Grandad

My grandad sits on a chair,
He only has a little bit of hair.
My grandad always falls asleep,
He probably dreams of riding in a jeep.
I have a grandad who is very lazy,
Sometimes we think he's going crazy.
He watches football all day
And then sits and stays.
He always takes the dog for a walk,
Also he likes to have a good talk.

Nicole Marsh (11)
Haughton Community School

My Backyard

There's a garage,
A path,
The rustling of trees close by,
The engines of cars far away,
Trees swaying, birds fluttering,
Sunny, sun shining, just the slightest breeze.
Summer, June, sunny midday,
The smooth feeling of the clean pavement.
The trees leaves rustle as the birds flutter down,
The vans parked outside the house.
Peter walks past,
I feel bored.
'Is there loads of trees where you live?'
'No just a couple.'
'No just a couple.'
A gate to open to go to the front of the house,
I wish I could go out there in the sun!

Nicola Hedley (12)
Haughton Community School

Mollie The Cat Is . . .

Trouble maker
Flea fluffer
Hairball maker
Make Dad hoover
Hair dropper
Horrible smeller
Food greeder
Can't stroke her
Quiet purrer
Not a hisser.

Callum Crackett (11)
Haughton Community School

Camera Con Vista

Blurred trees and bushes,
Maybe 1 or 2 cars,
A patterned drive and silver van,
The cars zoom past and the birds twitter,
The sun gleams through the fluffy clouds,
Lunchtime on a summer weekend.
Soft but bristly grass,
Smooth blue sky.
My neighbour's cat slips through a fence,
The wind scatters leaves everywhere.
My mum's car will soon enter the drive,
Feeling happy as the sun burns softly.
Who lives there?
The new people from London,
The new people from London.
The window sill I'm sitting on is smooth and warm,
I wish I could stay here forever.

Jessica McEwan (12)
Haughton Community School

On A School Morning

On a school morning
The sun's shining bright,
I must have slept all through the night.
I get ready for school,
Boy I look cool!
I go and meet my mates,
They're waiting at the gates.
We hear the bell,
We can tell
The teachers are coming,
Our brains are numbing,
The teachers give us a warning,
That's my school morning!

Abby Peverley (12)
Haughton Community School

Majorca

The sea is bright, with the sun setting on the horizon,
People walking back to hotels,
Cars zooming past,
Music playing loud, people laughing,
Birds flying back to their nests as night draws in,
The weather is cool after a long, hot day,
It's a summer evening,
The air is warm, but cooling down,
Buildings are getting cold after being warm,
There's a Spanish dog barking in the distance,
I know there are clouds, but I can't see them,
There's a thick black dust in the mountains,
It looks like a hurricane,
I feel scared with a hurricane flying past,
Why is this place full of people?
It's full because of the entertainment,
It's full because of the entertainment,
The hurricane is strong,
People still watching indoor entertainment,
I wish I could be in Majorca again.

Charlie Prendergast (12)
Haughton Community School

Lovers!

My lover gives me roses, lost upon the sky,
I need to know you better, before we even try.
Ohh baby, don't ignore me, listen to what I say,
Oh baby! Please, please stay.

So turn around and walk away, that's fine by me,
But don't expect to come back to a family.
Baby if you see me with another man,
That lover gave me roses better than you can.

Amy Foster & Emma Abernethy (13)
Haughton Community School

Countryside

A big, yellow combine harvester ploughing the field,
Mitzi, Penny and Tyson playing around,
The chickens clucking and scratching on the ground.
A blue tractor ploughing the field,
A fir tree swaying in the rain,
The rain was pouring down as it came,
November, autumn - winter is how it could be described.
I feel wet grass, soft under fur and the warmth of fresh eggs to eat.

A flock of seagulls or crows with bugs in the feet,
The feel of wind hitting the barn doors,
A thunderstorm is going to hit.
Boredom is setting in, with the rain we can't go out.

Why are the dogs, in the rain, playing about?
Because they want some fun and not to be stuck in all day.
Because they want some fun and not to be stuck in all day.
A big echo in the barn with the rain beating on the roof,
I wish it would stop raining.

Pauline Finney (12)
Haughton Community School

The Sea

The waves crash down upon the deep blue sea,
Sinking ships,
Drowning innocent people,
But most of all people ride the white stallions.

It's like a hand reaching out to touch the sand,
Getting closer and closer,
Nothing can beat its almighty strength,
Reaching out a great long length.

It floods towns,
It makes sheer tragedy,
It can run turbines with its strength,
Along an almighty length.

Ellis Hemmings (12)
Haughton Community School

The Perfect View

The misty hills glistening white, cornfields glowing gold.
Dead red roses, petalless tulips, a dull green bush,
The grumpy old man walking his dog,
As he trod to the field, whilst cars were passing by.
The trees blowing away from the wind.
The three-wheeler van which travels endlessly,
Raindrops falling on the ground, they're blowing heavily.
October, mucky autumn, puddles growing gradually,
On an early Saturday morning.
Rough pavement, stone, dead leaves feel crispy.
Birds eating the bread, a soft brown dog pulling its owner.
I hear a man walking towards me, a car beaming up the road.
I feel my mum is coming home,
I am anxious, nervous, feeling tired.
Does it always stay the same? Is it always so quiet?
It always stays the same, the noise changes over periods of time.
It always stays the same, the noise changes over periods of time.
My reflection in the clear window,
I wish, I wish, I was rich, forever and always.

Laura Pearson (12)
Haughton Community School

Chocolate

It clasps the tongue with dashing taste,
It glides down your throat like a sugary paste.

Some people don't like it, I love it though,
I could eat one bar or maybe even more.

You can get it in brown or white,
In my mouth it feels so lovely and light.

Chocolate is a dream come true,
Why not go buy some, yes I'm talking to you!

Kaleigh-Ann Swales (12)
Haughton Community School

A View From A Window

Cars covering two lanes of the road,
A row of houses on each side of the street,
Rain pattering down, sirens wailing far away,
Trees blowing, leaves falling and cars whizzing by.

Windy weather, rain flying toward the window,
A dull, dark afternoon in the middle of autumn,
If I were there, rain would splash on my hand
And bounce back on my face,
A bird's nest was hidden up in the tree above,
I can feel air breezing as the window is slightly open.

Neighbours run past with umbrellas, huddling into their jackets,
I feel cold as the breeze hits me,
Are you cozy in here?
Not really, it's so cold.
Not really, it's so cold.

I am in a red room,
I wish it was Christmas, time for snow.

Nicola Lodge (12)
Haughton Community School

The Stars

The stars twinkle like a flickering light,
Every child has their own shining bright.
I found it hard to find the right one,
Shining bright through the dark and dusky midnight sky.
I sat at my window looking right out,
To see where my shining light had made its travels to,
Only to find that, on the night that I sat looking out
I realised that my shining light had *gone!*

Hayley Allen (12)
Haughton Community School

Nature

Tips of large, green trees on the horizon.
Healthy, green grass and colourful flowers.
Kids screeching with laughter.
Engines from the nearby road.
Squirrels scurrying across the ground
Cold and damp outside.
Autumn, with radiant leaves across the ground.
Rough, sharp edges of walls.
Soft, shiny leaves sprawled across the grass,
Soft, furry squirrels digging their claws in as they go up the tree.
Kids having fun in the yard of the nearby school.
Crash of thunder as rain starts to pour.
Miserable and wet.
Where does that path lead to?
Nearby school and a supermarket where we all shop.
Nearby school and a supermarket where we all shop.
Warm, colourful, cosy bedroom,
I wish I was in a country where the sun is beaming down on me.

Zoe Thompson (12)
Haughton Community School

Registration

Mrs Corner's room, ten to nine,
The girls are gossiping,
The boys are on computers.
Daniel threw a bag across the room,
It hit Laura on the head,
She went bright red and started crying,
Books were scattered across the room,
Mr Jakson walked in
Everyone went silent.

Elizabeth Raper (13)
Haughton Community School

Bulgaria

Sunset in the distance.
Next door's balcony with a table and chairs.
People talking whilst sunbathing, waves clashing in the sea.
Palm trees swaying with the wind.
The sun is shining, it's scorching hot.
Summer, a July day in the mid afternoon.
The crispy bark on the palm trees.
A bird swooping down to catch its dinner.
The cafe downstairs, the clattering of the plates
From the dinners of people nearby.
My sister is just about to jump into the pool.
Feeling happy because I'm seeing people having a good time.
Can you get down to that beach?
Yes if you walk around the front of the hotel there are some steps.
Yes if you walk around the front of the hotel there are some steps.
My mam in the shower, I can hear the plip-plops of the water.
I wish to come back here again.

Charlotte Hall (12)
Haughton Community School

Tutor Time

In the teachers' lounge they meet,
It begins at 8.50 but the teachers cheat.
The girls put on make-up and do their hair,
The boys laugh, look and stare.
Craig did it in disgrace,
He hit the girl on her face.
She put her head up and then back down,
We all looked with a frown.
'Behave at once, this isn't a game,'
It was the head teacher, we all looked in shame.
We all realised it wasn't a game.

Danielle Ward (14)
Haughton Community School

My View

Fields, green and brown over in the distance,
A picnic table to the left in the corner of my garden.
The sound of birds in the trees,
Lorries and cars speeding down roads,
The waterfall of the pond, trickling down the rocky slope.
Cloudy, musty, it's hard to see into the distance,
It's afternoon, in autumn about 2 o'clock,
The cold spiky feel of the grass,
The rough feel of the tree trunk,
The outdoor cage of the guinea pig,
The small wet feet marks, evidence of birds,
My mum hanging out the washing, I know she is there.
Dad steps into view and starts up the lawnmower,
Happy but cold, the misty feeling makes me chilly,
'When do you look out to the view?'
'When I feel bored.'
'When I feel bored.'
A group of houses fading away into the distance.

Jane Armer (12)
Haughton Community School

Bullying

Bullying is a nasty thing,
Bullies may hit you or call you a ding.
The bullies may feel glad,
But we all know they are really sad.
Bullies will criticise you,
Just stand up for yourself, that's what I would do.
Take God's gift and express it as best as you can,
If you do you will have the best life ever
And you will get a tan.

Matthew Glenning (12)
Haughton Community School

Snowy Winter

Spire of St Cuthbert's painted in white,
Trees covered in snow, I wonder if it will snow again, it just might.
Both of my cats cold, miaowing at the door,
A robin flying to eat the bread on the floor.
White, cold and frosty on the far hill,
Children making the snow look like a windmill.
Lamp posts come on, so many lights,
Two children come out and start playing with kites.
Animals make tiny footprints in the snow,
Can't see animals but they are there, I know.
I feel warm next to the fire in my house,
Then running across the ground I see a mouse.
Every Christmas is it always like this?
Not always, but when it goes I will miss.
it should never melt! Never!
I wish it could stay forever.

Laura Pinder (12)
Haughton Community School

The Rain

Clink! Clink! goes the rain on the window,
Cars and people is what I see.
The rain makes me feel secure.
The window is freezing against my fingertips.
Hear the birds, I can hear the birds
But I can't see them.
All the cats hide except one.
I stretch out on my bed while waiting,
The game loads.
I read the mission objectives,
There is no rainbow,
There is no rainbow,
I feel happy that the rain has gone away,
The birds are coming in sight.

Jonathon Tweddle (13)
Haughton Community School

You're The One I Love!

Do you want to know how long we'll be lovers?
'Til the stars twinkle in the sky,
Until the water runs dry
And until the day I die.

I wrote your name in the sand,
But the waves washed it away.
I wrote your name in the clouds,
But the wind blew it away.
I wrote your name in my heart
And that's where it will stay.

Your name is precious,
It will never grow old,
It is engraved in my heart
With letters of *gold!*

Shamila Rahman (13)
Haughton Community School

Darlo Fan

Every weekend, no matter what the weather,
I go to watch Darlington
Who have recently got better.
If they keep this up
We'll get promoted
And get to the Premiership,
Well here's hoping!
The scream of the crowd,
'Foul ref, foul!'
Boos and hisses
All around the ground.
Darlington are losing,
We're back to normal.
Mid table mediocrity
Is the best we can do.

Liam Browne (11)
Haughton Community School

My Bear

Once there was a bear,
Who once had loads of hair.
He had a drink
And ate loads of ink,
Then he started to think.

Once there was a bear
Who tore up the bed.
He got told off, what a loss,
Then he wasn't the boss.

Hayley Hardman (11)
Haughton Community School

When The Sun Goes In

I made people smile all day long,
Sunbathing whilst singing a song,
In midday I shone even brighter,
Listening to gangs of laughter,
When suddenly I was overlapped
And then I got crowded and collapsed,
I'll just have to wait for another morning.

Sara Dobson (11)
Haughton Community School

African Documentary

Giant hose protrudes from mouth,
Enormous loads come out south,
Vast grey, bulging belly,
Frequently seen in nature films on telly,
What am I?

Philip Bayles (11)
Haughton Community School

My Family

M ake me smile when I am down,
Y ou never make me frown.

F rom all the years we have had
A lways been good and never bad,
M y life has been the best these years,
 I f I ever have a problem you are there,
L iving my problems for me.
Y ou are the best, you are my family!

Samantha Herrington (13)
Haughton Community School

Snowman

S oft snowy friend,
N ever stays forever,
O nly likes cold so it can survive,
W et and cold like an ice cube,
M ade of snow.
A lways left to melt over night,
N ose like a carrot.

Karl Wake (11)
Haughton Community School

Macbeth

M acbeth had some friends
A nd they told him some things,
C razy he went,
B ut he killed a king,
E xtraordinarily he became the high one.
T he newly elected king killed all his mates,
H e now sits alone on his lonely throno.

Daniel Barber (13)
Haughton Community School

Friendship

K ind and caring in every way,
A lways here to save the day,
T hen all you need to do is see I'm
H ere for all the times you need me. The
R ough, good and the bad,
Y ou only need to know I'm here for when you're sad.
N ow all you need to do is call on me to see you through.

S ometimes I may need you.
M aybe you will help me like I'll help you,
I 'll be here till the day I die,
T ill there's nothing left at all,
H ere for you always.

Kathryn Smith (13)
Haughton Community School

Tennis

T he ball bouncing,
E very one pouncing,
N ever-ending balls appear as the players start to fear,
N never-ending cheers,
I nches of tarmac eroding,
S houtings and screamings as the game ends.

Hannah Holden (11)
Haughton Community School

It's A Tough Life

S tupid is what my parents call me,
C an't see why though?
O ver and over, it gets
T ougher and tougher, now
T hey shall pay.

Scott Banner (14)
Haughton Community School

My Window View

In the distance I can see a forest that stretches as far as I can see,
In the left foreground I can see next door's dog barking
                                              as mad as can be.
The nearest sound I can hear is next door's dog barking wildly,
The furthest sound I can hear is the birds chirping loudly.
I can see the wind blowing softly upon the leaves.
The time is 6.30, the season is autumn, day Friday.
I can see beautifully coloured leaves, I can feel the wind,
I can see a movement, probably a bird.
What is hidden is the wind that can be felt.
I can see a thunderstorm on the horizon!
I am thinking the wood is in danger of fire,
The guest says, 'Are you bored of this scenery?'
I look shocked and say, 'No.'
The guest says, 'What you need is some city life.'
I can see on the inside of the woods that there is lots of adventure.
I wish that everyone would appreciate the forest.

Natasha Campbell (12)
Haughton Community School

Truth Hurts

I felt so alone, I felt so scared,
I knew that no one ever cared,
Why had I been so stupid?
Why did I do what I did?

I thought it was right, but it was wrong,
Now that I sing, a tuneless song,
It was all a lie, it was never true,
You didn't love me but I loved you.

But I moved on ever so fast
And found my one true love at last!
I'll never forget my time with you
But you will forget your time with me.

Amanda Dixon (11)
Haughton Community School

Looking Out Of The Window

Houses and tree tops spreading thousands of miles,
Children playing and laughing,
The sound of laughing, blocking out the sound of shouting,
Trees swaying backwards and forwards, side to side.
The weather, bright sunshine,
Around lunchtime, around summer.
Soft and spiky,
A dog (a runner) in the garden opposite lounging in the sun,
Hope I can't see it but I know it is there.
The dog gets excited, the children are now having a water fight.
I feel so lonely, I want to go out,
But I can't.
Why are you standing there?
Just looking at the view,
Just looking at the view.
I feel so lonely,
I wish I was out there too.

Jamie-Ann Donald (12)
Haughton Community School

Registration

B-23 at 5 to 9,
The girls are chatting all the time.
The boys are loud in the afternoon,
Because one of the boys across the room
Aimed a bag at Thomas Bloom,
It hit a girl called Rachel Black,
With all the desks laid on their back.
The teacher yelled, 'Sort them out.'
Then suddenly in came Mr Sprout.
The girls shut up,
The boys sat down,
They all looked at him
And thought what a clown.

Craig Hart (13)
Haughton Community School

Pollution Poem

Pollutant in the river,
Pollutant in the sea,
Pollutant in the river,
That's not the life for me.
Tankers in Dover
May tip over,
Pollutants in the sea from both you and me,
Affect our world in some way.
Once a land of glory
Now tells us a story,
That pollutant will kill
And will also fill
The world with poisonous gas.
Fish are dying all the time
From waste and grime,
It's up to you and me
To save our world and sea.

Carl Hardman (12)
Haughton Community School

The View

Houses and buildings stretching far away,
A long, blue river with London's famous landmarks.
The noise of the plane as it flies through the air,
The soft, white clouds passing by.
The golden sun is rising above the misty horizon.
The plane is just about to land,
I am happy and very excited.
I wish my mum, dad and nana
Could see this beautiful view.

Gareth McShane (14)
Haughton Community School

Love

You remind me of a rose
blooming from the ground.

You remind me of passion,
romance and no sound.

You remind me of sugar,
so sweet and kind.

24/7 you are always
on my mind.

So don't forget me
while you're gone.

I miss you, you know,
please don't be too long.

Amy Foster (12)
Haughton Community School

As Dull As Rain

The rain is tapping on my window,
I see a dark, grey, gloomy sky.
The day is dull just like me,
I look out my window
And see nothing more than clouds.
I stretch out on my bed,
I pick up my magazine and start to read.
The rain gets slower and then it stops.
The sky is lightening
And there is a rainbow.
I see my three favourite colours,
Red, yellow and blue.
My lips create a smile
And I see birds flying.

Hayley Brady (13)
Haughton Community School

Starfish

It lives under a greeny-blue place,
It never makes a single sound,
It's so peaceful and quiet.
It smells like an ingredient
You would use in a pie.
It feels scaly and cold,
It looks yellowy-gold,
It gives you a warm feeling of happiness.

What am I?

Annabel Townsend (11)
Haughton Community School

My Uncle

My uncle died not long ago,
The sad feelings are there and will not go,
Day after day time passes by,
All I want to do is sit and cry,
Seeing his grave and taking flowers
But always leaving in big tear showers,
After all this sadness I have to move on,
I just can't stand the fact he's gone.

Rebecca Mills (13)
Haughton Community School

Vera

There was an old lady called Vera,
She always got mixed up and used Lira,
If you were her good old friend
You'd be round the bend,
Just don't compete with Vera.

Amy Wearmouth (14)
Haughton Community School

The View From A Window

Back of houses from the other street,
Grass in my garden,
Birds singing and cars going past on the busy road,
Birds flying from tree to tree,
Bright hot sun shining down, glistening on the parked cars.
Summer, July afternoon,
A sign of bird feathers left behind.
A car coming down the road.
I feel happy because it is a summer's day.
What is happening out here?
The birds are singing loudly,
The birds are singing loudly,
I see glass,
I wish it never ends.

Christina Hauxwell (13)
Haughton Community School

Registration

Computer room,
10 minutes to 9 o'clock.
Chatting,
Chatting,
Matthew threw the bag across the room.

No one,
You are stupid.
The desk fell over,
'Detention,' the teacher shouted.
'Teacher, teacher.'
'Silence, silence,
Why did you do that?'

Mark Hall (13)
Haughton Community School

Bedroom Window

Dull white garages, bright gardens.
My garden and my garage.
Hammering and birds singing.
Willows swaying in the garden.
Sunny and light breeze.
Autumn just coming, dark.
Soft mud and rough decking,
Glass smooth table.
Birds food dropping, flying across the house.
Gardeners turn the radio up.
Happy and calm because of the birds singing.
What are you getting done in your garden?
I am cutting grass and the decking's done.
I am cutting grass and the decking's done.
I can see my bed,
I wish that I could get my room redecorated.

Nicole Atkins (13)
Haughton Community School

Old People

I don't like old people,
Most of them just moan.
If there's one bit of trouble
They are straight onto the phone.

Play football near their houses,
They go in a mood.
Then they tell our parents
And they tell us off too.

All we want to do
Is play our game.
Why can't you leave us alone?
So we can play again!

Billy Mee (13)
Haughton Community School

In The Presence Of Evil

Here he is, here he lies,
Nobody laughs, nobody cries.
How he feels and how he fares,
No one knows and no one cares.

Now he lies in eternal rest,
He's suffered the worst, he's suffered the best.
But hadn't fate shown his face
He'd still be in a far worse place.

The moral of the story is,
This twisted, fickle tale of his.
Evil in life, evil in death,
Here lies the corpse of King Macbeth.

Ben Reidy (13)
Haughton Community School

Loving Forever

Just two months ago my dad died,
For days and days I just cried.
I think about him all the time,
Even when the sun don't shine.
Through wind and rain, sun and snow,
I love him more than you will know.
In my heart we'll be together,
Loving him more, always and forever.

Time's passed by, but still I cry,
Whenever I'm alone
When thinking about my father's death,
I wish he would come home.

Kara Reed (13)
Haughton Community School

The Tudors

The barber's doing surgery,
Not cutting people's hair.
The King's chopping people's heads,
The reason is not fair.

Death by hanging, death by chopping,
Being burnt alive.
You are really lucky
If you can survive.

The scurvy and the plague,
The sweat and things much worse.
If this was someone's normal life,
Imagine being cursed.

Today is a lot kinder
Than those awful times.
You can only read about it,
Or listen to my rhymes.

Terri Stephens (11)
Haughton Community School

I Dream Of Love

I do not have a love life
I dream of
Me and my love together.

There she walks, my one true love,
My only
Wish, for her to stay with me.

But I know I am dreaming,
She will not
Be mine. Only in my dreams.

Craig Stephens (13)
Haughton Community School

The Ocean

The crashing against the rocks,
The whispering against children's ankles,
The splash of waving arms and legs,
The *ploge* of a bucket splodging in the water.

The roar of the waves,
The whistle of the wind,
The ear-piercing echo of the empty coves and caves,
As the water comes closer.

The squawking of seagulls,
The bubbles of fish,
Up for the chase, swimming away,
Faster! Faster! Faster,
Until . . .

Gulp . . . as a bigger fish has its feed,
Chewing, coughing on a bone,
Swimming away on a full stomach
And then the sunny sky disappears,
And black fills the sky,
Until the next day the sea sleeps soundly.

This is the full example of a day at the ocean!

Jessica Sandiford (11)
Haughton Community School

The Mad Teacher

She's mad, she's sad
And sends you out,
If you speak in her classroom.
When you enter you're
Scared to even breathe,
In case she gives you detention.

Samantha Colbeck (11)
Haughton Community School

The View

Tiny boats on the seas horizon,
People splashing in the pool down below.
Seagulls croaking in the distance,
People on the beach having fun.
Sun gleaming and heating the ground.
It's just gone midday in the middle of summer,
The sand is soft, the sea has gentle waves flowing in and out.
The fish are swimming swiftly in the sea.
There's an ice cream parlour, I just can't see it.
Big waves are coming,
I wish I was down there.
How long do you stay here?
2 days longer?
2 days longer?
There is a no smoking sign,
I wish my dad would win the lottery.

Matthew Wain (12)
Haughton Community School

Starting A New School

Going to Haughton, just starting year seven,
I'm just going to tell you this is not Heaven!
All those people staring at you,
Straight away they can tell that you are new!
Trying to fit in can be so tough,
Lots of older kids acting all rough.
Some of the lessons can seem very hard,
It's a relief when you're with your mate in the yard.
The school's so big, the year eleven's are so tall,
Compared to everything else I'm so small.
When you get in it's a relief,
You can stop worrying, no more grief!
But tomorrow, another school day will come,
No one to run to, not even your mum!

Rebekah Morgan (11)
Haughton Community School

My Horse - Bracken

My horse he is called Bracken,
He's very special to me.
All I want out of life
Is to have him home for tea.

When I asked my mam,
She said, 'Niki, no, no, no, no, no.'
But when she went out shopping,
I said, 'Come on Bracken, lets go, go, go, go, go.'

When Mam arrived back home, Bracken was having tea,
And when she walked through the door,
With shock she fell down to her knee.

'Mam,' I said, 'I'm sorry.'
Mam looked and smiled at me,
'Niki,' she said, 'I forgive you,
Because he means just as much to me.'

Nikita McNiff (11)
Haughton Community School

Registration Rumpus

We're in a building at ten to nine,
The girls are doing the only thing they can do, chat,
While the boys play cards, Perri nicks Jonny's bag
And launches it at Luke.

Luke starts to cry,
Everyone starts to laugh.
Perri acts like he never did anything.
The teacher yells get out!
While Perri walks out, someone walks in.
Who is it? Grey hair, it's an old woman, why is she here?
It's Perri's gran, she starts hugging and kissing him.
Everyone laughs at him,
Ha! Ha!

Richard Holt (13)
Haughton Community School

What Am I?

I once lived underwater,
Been put through awful slaughter,
My colours may vary,
I could have lived in Tipperary,
I only have five
And I wish I had nine,
I have no face,
What a disgrace.
I move slowly
And hide lowly,
What am I?

Answer: starfish.

Samantha Beckham (11)
Haughton Community School

Registration

Monday morning in a classroom,
Time is 8.50,
Girls chatting,
Boys chatting,
Sam threw a bag, as usual
Shaun threw it back.
Desks moved here, there and everywhere,
'Stop!' shouted the teacher.
Mr Thomas came in,
'Everyone shut up.'
I whispered, 'He never smiles.'

Natalie Taylor (14)
Haughton Community School

Lace - My Horse

Lace Is a grey,
Nearly 8,
She is nice to ride
And is a mate.

She and I are
Such very good friends,
I hope this friendship
Never ends.

She eats her oats
From a purple pail,
And eats her hay
From a fresh bale.

Over the fields
And far away,
Me and my horse
Go out to play.

Becky Stephenson (11)
Haughton Community School

The Lion Poem

Lion senses men and horses,
Sniffs the air,
Sniffs then pauses.

A stink he thinks
Normally there,
An animal somewhere on his land.

Then the lion stares at the antelope,
In the bush he stalks the antelope.
Then he chases his prey
Until the end of the day.

Dean McShane (12)
Haughton Community School

Me

J enna is my name but
E veryone calls me Jen, I say
N o to rain, I say
N o to bad weather altogether!
A solicitor or bar manager is what I want to

B e!
E njoy wearing the latest fashions, I
L ike to shop, shop, shop!
L ove parties, Christmas and my boyfriend, Michael.

Jenna Bell (13)
Haughton Community School

I Can't Remember . . .

I can't remember who left a floater in the loo.
I can't remember what it's like to do squat.
I can't remember why rain falls from the sky.
I can't remember when I last saw a hen.
I can't remember where I used to wash my hair.
I can't remember whether I've still got my feather.
I can't remember how we get milk from a cow.
I can't remember if my cat is called Riff.

Joe Lythe (12)
Haughton Community School

My Poem Life

I am Lauren, I like to dance,
I like my music but I don't like trance,
I like a chance to dance,
I don't mind rave,
But my mum's boyfriend is called Dave.

Lauren Risbrough (11)
Haughton Community School

The View

Children playing in the park,
Laughing and having fun.
Flowers in the garden getting ready to bloom.
In the distance kids having fun,
TV blaring out.
Shep running in the garden,
Barking at any kids going by.
Black clouds hanging, the sun peeping through
Feeling the grass, just to be home again
Away from England.
Squirrels bopping about looking for nuts,
Feeling of love and happiness all around.
Banging as the army practise,
Happy to see my mum where she belongs, at home.
Do you like the view? What do you see?

Yes, you see everyone happy,
Yes, you see everyone happy.
My bed lying there,
I wish this would never end.

Kerry Sweeten (14)
Haughton Community School

Registration

In a room,
8.50,
Talking,
Playing on computers,
Lewis shot a bag across the room,
The bag hit Laura,
Stuff got knocked off,
Teacher shouts, 'Stop it now.'
Mr Thomas walks in,
Suddenly went quiet,
Going to get told off.

Sarah Greaves (13)
Haughton Community School

Nana (My Number 2 After My Mam)

Nana, Nana
She's always here.
Nana, Nana
She can appear from nowhere.

Nana, Nana
I love her lots.
Nana, Nana
She gets me out of tight spots.

She's here and there,
She always cares,
She buys me everything,
She's like a cuddly teddy bear.

Nana, Nana
She loves me lots.
Nana, Nana
She loves washing pots.

Nana, Nana
I love her too.
Nana, Nana
She can be my number 2.

Stephanie Bene (12)
Haughton Community School

Kim

Young Kim would not go to bed,
But sat watching TV instead.
As she stayed to stare,
Her face went all square,
And aerials grew from her hair.
As her family all went to sleep,
Downstairs Kim did creep,
And if you want to know why,
Downstairs is where they had Sky.

Kimberley Stokes (12)
Haughton Community School

Zebra

I saw a zebra
Two days old,
His head was too big
For his neck to hold.
His legs were shaky
And thin and loose,
They rocked and swayed
And weren't much use.

He tried to run
And jumped a bit,
But he wasn't quite sure
How to do it.
His queer fur coat
Was black and white,
Stripy and shiny,
A beautiful sight.

He looked so small
And frail and slim.
I hoped everyone
Would be good to him.

Scott Barraclough (12)
Haughton Community School

Turtle

I feel like hiding in my shell,
But I know I have to be brave.
I feel scared and frightened,
But I know I have to be tough.
I feel like I'm not me anymore,
But I know I have to remember.
I know it should be easy,
Deep down I'm me.

Stacey Brocklebank (11)
Haughton Community School

Doug The Thug

There once was a boy named Doug
Who was a notorious thug,
He lived in a bin
And ate scraps for his din,
But dessert was always a bug.

He was happy like this
And life was bliss,
Until a new law was passed.
Now all homeless thugs
Get stuck working tugs,
Unless they can find a real job.

William Parkinson (14)
Haughton Community School

If I Told You How I Feel

If I told you how I feel
Would you turn and walk away?

If I told you how I feel
Would you tell me that you love me too?

But if you said you hated me,
I would cry until the Earth has died.

I would be lost without you
There is no world without you.

If you turned your back on me
The sun wouldn't shine.

I need you to survive
But if you're not there I will die.

Siân Sunley (13)
Hurworth School - Maths & Computing College

The Seasons

The flowers dance,
The lambs prance,
All the birds sing,
They dance and they prance,
This is spring.

The sunlight dreams,
All playing kids scream,
Summer is here,
It dreams and they scream,
School holidays are near.

The leaves die,
The fireworks fly,
The nights draw in,
They fly and they die,
They make a din.

The snowflake falls,
The cold air calls,
It keeps the animals at bay,
It falls and calls,
Then it fades away.

Rhys Whitney (13)
Hurworth School - Maths & Computing College

If I Told You How I Feel

If I told you how I feel,
Would you push me away?
Would you laugh at me
And tell everyone what I say?

If I asked you, 'Would you go out with me?'
Would you laugh and turn away?

Jessica Kelly (13)
Hurworth School - Maths & Computing College

How I Feel

If I told you how I feel,
Would you feel it deep down?
If I told you how I feel,
Would you seize that love?

If I told you how I feel,
Would you be that same person?
If I told you how I feel,
Would you say the truth?

If I told you how I feel,
Would that love stay between us?
If I told you how I feel,
Would you treat me just the same?

If I told you how I feel,
Would you be angry?
If I told you how I feel,
Would you still be my magic wonder?

Rebecca Ann Edwards (11)
Hurworth School - Maths & Computing College

If I Told You How I Feel

If I told you how I feel,
Would you listen to me?
All my thoughts and feelings for you would fill you with glee,
I hate it when you have to go away to work and say goodbye,
Because when I really need you, you're not with me so I'm upset
And start to cry,
But when you are with me I love it when you call me pet,
Until that time comes again that fills me with threat,
If I told you how I feel,
Would you tell me it's OK,
So that we could sit on the couch and watch the telly all day.

Sophie Carvell (11)
Hurworth School - Maths & Computing College

If I Told You How I Feel

If I told you how I feel,
Would you laugh or cry
Or turn around to me and tell me the same?
You are my guardian angel,
Always watching over me.

You are always there for me,
Through my happy and sad times,
And I am there for you,
Through your happy and sad times,
For I am your sister, you are my brother.

You maybe more clever than me,
And older too,
But deep down inside of you,
You are like me too,
A human being.

You're like a star,
Always bright and never depressed,
And only shine when it is time,
You never seem to be sad,
Or scared of anything.

But one thing I'm scared of, about happening to you,
Is that you will walk out that door into the world,
And never ever come back,
All those mean things I have said to you,
I don't mean it,
And I don't mean to embarrass you.

So when I come home and see you there,
I will leave you in peace,
Be nice to you, be a friend to you,
You know I would do anything for you,
This is how I feel.

Laura Carter (12)
Hurworth School - Maths & Computing College

The Staircase To Where?

Like a coiled snake staircase,
An infinity-sided shape,
Doors are doors,
Windows are windows,
But what are stairs?
They are betroved to the maze,
A shadow of doom lurks in every corner,
Faceless goblins scatter the maze.

As soon as they walk in the nightmare will begin,
A plastic world that doesn't sleep,
Or even exist,
Even the plants are frozen in time,
Not affected by gravity,
Solemn but yet alive,
A Rubik's cube of mystery,
Each door is leading to a different world,
A wheel of doom lies behind every door,
For all who enter there is no more.

Chris Smith (12)
Hurworth School - Maths & Computing College

If I Told You How I Feel

If I told you how I feel
Would you be shocked or surprised?
I love you more than anyone
You're the most special thing of all
You've made my dreams come true
All I want is you
You're the only thing I think about
So please! Please! Be the one.
Me and you can have miracles
But all you have to do is be the one.

Melissa Causer (11)
Hurworth School - Maths & Computing College

If I Told You How I Feel, Ember

If I told you how I feel,
You wouldn't understand,
You walk on all fours,
And I walk around and stand.

It's like we speak a different language,
But I'm sure you listen to me,
I think you'd rather do something else though,
Like chase a cat round a tree.

I love the way you come to me,
And give me your paw,
When I tickle your belly,
You dance around the floor.

But now that you are poorly,
I will help you through,
You are great Ember,
And I love you.

Laura Crawford (12)
Hurworth School - Maths & Computing College

If I Told You How I Feel

If I told you how I feel,
Would you laugh
Or would you look away and smile?

If I told you how I feel,
Would you stare in wonder
Or would you wait in curiosity?

Feelings or no feelings,
There is no other way
Look to both sides, you will find
That there is nothing there.

Gemma Eddy (12)
Hurworth School - Maths & Computing College

Summer

Summer is here,
The best time of all,
Relaxing to temptation,
Having a ball.

The bright yellow sun,
The people will scream,
When their tan begins to burn,
Then, they'll cool down with a nice, tasty ice cream.

'Yes' the children shout with joy,
As they are released from school for loads of days,
They're going home to do some more packing,
As soon they're going on their holidays.

Thank goodness for summertime,
Everyone's having fun with all their friends,
At the seaside, 'let's buy an ice cream,'
All having fun till the summer finally ends.

Summer is over,
It was the best time of all,
Relaxed to temptation,
Had a ball.

Sabriye Wallis (13)
Hurworth School - Maths & Computing College

My Dog

If I told you how I feel,
It would make you feel cool,
You are the best dog I ever had
That's why I named you Sam.
I dread to think about bad things
That could happen to you, but it gives me joy
To think of the good things,
So thanks for being you
And carry on being my best dog.

Lee Marshall (11)
Hurworth School - Maths & Computing College

The Cat

The friendly cat all black and white
She drinks the milk with all her might
She wanders here and there
In the pleasant open air

In winter she is lost in snow
And wet with all the showers
She walks among the long grass
In any kind of weather

All wet with snow and as cold as ice
She likes to lie by the fire
Curled up tight nice and warm
Ready to say night night!

Lauren Mitchell (14)
Hurworth School - Maths & Computing College

Love And Hate

I hate the way you lie to me,
I hate it when you shout.
I hate it when you say you'll be there,
You make me feel left out.

I love the way you cuddle me,
I love you when you care.
I love you when you watch over me,
I love you when you're there.

I hate you when you hit me,
I hate you when you steal.
I love you when you're here,
You're always there for me.

Jennifer Mitchell (13)
Hurworth School - Maths & Computing College

Match Day

First you decide if you are going
Your favourite player may be Owen.
Then you go to buy your ticket.
When you have got it you will be glad.

You're inside the stadium, it is loud.
You think they're going to win
But you don't know how.
You get to your seat
You crank up the heat,
By singing a brand new song.

Your favourite player is not there
You think it's really unfair
You want them to - play
But it may not be their day.

Yes! the first goal has gone in
From a throw-in
Now you're one-nil up
So you will win the cup.

The final whistle has just gone
Now your team is number one
Now you have won the cup
And told all the critics to shut right up!

Chris Oakley (14)
Hurworth School - Maths & Computing College

Slipper

There once was a lady who lived in a slipper
She only had one little nipper.
One day her family decided it just wouldn't do
So the council moved her to a shoe
She's very happy in the shoe
But the little nipper
Wants to move back to the slipper.

Christina Naylor (12)
Hurworth School - Maths & Computing College

This World

People come
People go
In and out
And so and so.

That's what it's like in this world.

Wives love men
Men love wives
If not too busy
With their own lives.

That's what it's like in this world.

People too busy
With themselves
They put their friends
Upon the shelves.

That's what it's like in this world.

This world's cracked up
I tell you so
But no doubt now
You've got to go.

That's what it's like in this world.

Stuart Read (12)
Hurworth School - Maths & Computing College

Savage Sharks

Savage sharks
With hungry appetites
Silently swim
Attacking with surprise
Massive teeth
Grind, crunch and kill
Always hungry
Searching for food.

Jack Heseltine (12)
Hurworth School - Maths & Computing College

Love

If I told you how I feel,
If I opened my heart and expressed my feelings . . .
I don't want us to part
If I could turn back the clock, it would just be the same.
I like you more than a good football game.
I'm out with the lads playing football again.
I'll see you after it starts to rain.
I'm sorry I can't see you, things just aren't the same.
There's something I don't like about you,
But I can't tell you, it will give you a fright!
But hold on a minute! I've just woken up.
It was only a dream, me and you are just not the same.
This dream will not come true.
This makes me really sad.
I spent the night in my bed dreaming of you,
There's nothing more to be said.

Lewis Longstaff (11)
Hurworth School - Maths & Computing College

Morning

A small glass cylinder stands alone,
With grains of salt for company.
Slowly a tail bats the air as a feline wanders outside
Gracefully she walks along the concrete path
To the sweet smelling grass
To hide in the rose bush.
I watch a little while, she tries to catch a buzzing bee,
She leaps gracefully, but a dog barks.
I pick up a frightened feline from the hard kitchen floor.
I stroke her fur, her fur soft as silk.
I Pick up a frightened feline from the hard kitchen floor.
Life is wonderful, this is a wonderful life.

Megan Keen (13)
Hurworth School - Maths & Computing College

Moles

Moles live in holes,
they eat worms,
they squeak and scamper like a soft cushion hitting a wall,
they nibble and chew,
sleep when it is cold,
they build tunnels far, far along,
but they always get along.
If they are threatened,
they are most fierce,
their claws are sharp,
just like a blade,
but if they are cared for they are so good.
Just remember they are just moles,
not territorial like cats,
they share land and food,
but if they are threatened they go underground,
far along,
for it is so safe and warm for them,
but just remember they are just moles,
just soft, furry moles.

Stephen Duncan (13)
Hurworth School - Maths & Computing College

If I Told You How I Feel

If I told you how I feel would you be amazed,
Or would you feel confused or even slightly dazed?
I know I should tell you this more often than I do,
I love you Mum and I always will do too.
I know I scream and shout a lot when you tell me off,
But you are always there for me when I sneeze and cough,
You are really special to me,
And I promise you always will be,
So thank you Mum for being there,
Even if I am really hard to bear.

Jade Hall (13)
Hurworth School - Maths & Computing College

My Brother Lucas

I have a brother called Lucas,
He is four years old.
He has blond hair and blue eyes,
To primary school he goes.

He loves Spider-man and Power Rangers,
He's mad, funny and cute,
With his best friend Aaron,
He drives my mam through the roof.

I love my brother Lucas,
Being a big sis is great,
And hopefully,
We will always stay good mates.

Jenna Hutchinson (13)
Hurworth School - Maths & Computing College

My Little Puppy

My furry lonely little puppy,
Sits happily beside the fire,
My furry lonely little puppy,
Slowly starting to tire.

My furry lonely little puppy,
Looking straight at me,
My furry lonely little puppy,
Wanting, wanting tea.

My furry lonely little puppy,
Happy as could be,
My furry lonely little puppy,
Loving, loving me . . .

Jonathan Weeks
Hurworth School - Maths & Computing College

The Ultimate Rhyme

One was mean,
One was lean,
The other was fat and mean.

They caught a fly,
But they couldn't remember why
So they let it die.

They went to catch a rat,
Each was carrying a bat,
And wearing a hat.

They went to talk to a man,
He was called Dan,
They went in their van.

They are off to see Godzilla,
That big killer,
But they were stopped by a gorilla.

They are going to climb a tree,
Where they will be free,
But had to wait for Jim to have a pee.

They went to do a bank job,
But they were caught by the mob,
Now they are in prison with Bob.

One was mean, but not no more,
One was lean, but not no more,
The other was fat and mean, but not no more.

They are going to fry,
They are going to die,
All this from an electric chair,
Or was it a bear?
I couldn't really care.

Andrew Sanderson (13)
Hurworth School - Maths & Computing College

If I Told You How I Feel

If I told you how I feel would you tell on me?
Might you finally see?

Would you listen to my face
Or simply run away in haste?

You always hit me when no one's there,
You scratch me, pinch me, pull my hair.

You fall over and cut your knee,
Then tell Mum and blame it on me!

When we argue you're far too quick,
I can't keep up so am forced to kick!

You're everyone's favourite, it's clear to see,
But no one ever makes a fuss over me!

You're not such a bad brother but for some things you do,
Like picking your nose and eating the goo!

Sometimes I wish you were gone with a simple touch!
But then I would miss you far too much!

Hannah Barron (12)
Hurworth School - Maths & Computing College

If I Told You How I Feel

If I told you how I feel
You would not believe me,
I know I am not as kind as you
As I should be
But you're my brother and you're the real deal.

You care for me and help me,
You are a lot stronger than me,
You are a lot wiser than me.

Alexander Glasper (12)
Hurworth School - Maths & Computing College

The Storm

High in the sky, away to the west,
The threatening storm clouds loom,
While down on the ground, people rush home,
Amidst the gathering gloom.

Before too long the heavens part
And heavy rain pours down,
It runs in streams along the road
And bounces off the ground.

A rumbling echo fills the sky,
The thunder bangs and crashes,
Like spears thrown from dark grey clouds,
The lightning strikes and flashes.

Along the path an old math struggles
Against the battling gale,
His bending umbrella swoops and soars
Away on the wind it sails.

A break appears in the murky clouds,
A glimmer of light shines through,
The storm rages on, no mercy shown
For neither me nor you.

The rain slows down and fades away,
As it hits the sodden ground,
The clouds begin to drift apart,
And the sun shines bright all around.

Catherine Hodgson (13)
Hurworth School - Maths & Computing College

If I Told You How I Feel

If I told you how I feel would you listen with pride,
Or would you stamp your feet?
Be ashamed and hide.

You see I really want to tell you something,
Something stuck in my mind,
Over all the years I have known you,
You have been nothing but kind.

You are there when I need you,
A shoulder for support,
A gentle look of lovingness,
Is achieved without thought.

This is my way of showing you,
With mutual pride,
You're the world's greatest sister,
I could ever find.

Sarah Kitching (12)
Hurworth School - Maths & Computing College

Adam The Best Little Bro In Every Way

If I told you how I feel,
Would you be surprised?
Would you turn and shrug
Or gasp and shut your eyes?

If you ran away
I would look for you day and night,
If I found you in a ditch, dead,
I would be in fright.

I would bury you in the best way,
I would send you away with tears in my eyes,

You are the best little bro in every way,
I hope you are with me to the end of my days.

Jonathan Snowden (13)
Hurworth School - Maths & Computing College

Jealousy

If I told you how I feel,
I'm sure you wouldn't understand,
Which is why I try to keep my feelings,
All bottled up inside.
It makes me feel inadequate
'Cause you're so popular at school,
You don't have my cares or worries,
Like trying to look cool.
You're pretty and you're clever,
You're all I'll never be,
I'll always be the plain one,
And you - leagues ahead of me.
When I go in for a cuddle,
You never have the time,
You've other things to do,
Or 'go away' you'll mime.
You don't talk to me in public . . .
At least no louder than a whisper,
You're embarrassed to be seen with me,
Despite being my little sister.

Sophie Miller (12)
Hurworth School - Maths & Computing College

My Poem

If I told you how I feel
Would you dance around in joy
Or would you go and punch Roy?
Would you slap him in the face
Or stroll down the street in grace?
I know that sometimes you hate me,
And then sometimes you hit me,
But I just hope that maybe
You'll grow up and start to like me.

Adam Walton (12)
Hurworth School - Maths & Computing College

If I Told You How I Feel

If I told you how I feel,
I doubt you'd be surprised,
Because I've told you loads of times,
It's your attitude I despise.

No matter how much mud I throw,
It never seems to stick,
And no matter what the comeback,
Yours is boring but it's quick.

And whenever a fight gets out of hand,
You seem to let it pass,
But you cry when I'm not looking,
And you run to Mum to grass.

You never do anything unless you'll win,
You'll whinge and whine and yell,
And you'll get your friends to make up trash,
And make my life like hell.

Sometimes I think that you're a whiny little brat,
And you never managed to ever get past three,
And I sometimes think that if you were my furry little pet,
Outside is where you'd definitely be.

But sometimes I think that you're really quite OK,
And we can actually get along quite fine,
And even though we fight like cat and dog, I can still say,
That you're not a perfect sister but you're mine.

Joshua Brennan (12)
Hurworth School - Maths & Computing College

Cracked Up, Smacked Up

Cracked up,
Smacked up,
Lying on the floor,
What was it I was looking for?
A way to escape, a way to let go,
I am no more that average Joe.

Cracked up,
Smacked up,
What am I worth?
The black, the death, this hopeless mirth,
All I live for lies in my hand,
And now I'm off to the promised land.

Cracked up,
Smacked up,
To Earth I return,
I am sure I have taken the wrong turn,
This dangerous world I opened the door,
I invited it in and screamed for more.

Cracked up,
Smacked up,
My life was once carefree,
The only danger now is me,
But I will kill me or it will,
Either way the answer lies in a pill.

Brogan May Hendry (12)
Hurworth School - Maths & Computing College

The Forest

The floor is a crisp duvet of leaves,
A river curves like a slithering snake,
Flowers decorate like beautiful wreaths,
The water glistens in the dazzling sunshine.

Wildlife scurries freely across the ground,
The forest is a paradise untouched by humans,
Up, down and around,
Everywhere you look animals play like leaves in the wind.

Trees stand bold, towering and protecting what lies below,
Hiding the treasures of pure Heaven,
Friends of the fellow,
Are welcome here.

Creatures ponder,
Busy and trouble free,
Don't stop to wonder,
All nature's secrets put into their homes.

As night becomes day the creatures play,
A fearless dance,
Everyone will stay,
But don't stop now,
We hear them shout, 'There's work to be done.'

Vicky Ramsden
Hurworth School - Maths & Computing College

My Puppy

My puppy's sparkling eyes
Beg for a stroke,
Lying on her tummy,
She wriggles her paws in joy,
Sitting at the door crying to go outside,
Lying there on the floor with her smiley grin,
Her padded paws press against my face,
So smooth, so soft, so gentle.

Sian Hill (12)
Hurworth School - Maths & Computing College

Sister

If I told you how I feel,
Would you hug me tight and squeeze,
If I looked you in the eyes,
Or I got down on my knees.

You fight and argue with me,
Or just ignore my words,
You are angry if I bring round friends,
And call them freaky nerds.

I argue back or pull a face,
But sometimes sit and cry,
Because I love you deep inside,
And to show you I do try.

It never works,
You don't understand,
We don't do things together,
Or even hold hands.

It's not a dream,
But could still come true,
If I told the truth,
That I'm worried about you.

Elizabeth Doubleday (12)
Hurworth School - Maths & Computing College

Feelings

Life can bring you down
Meaning that you're sad.
Sometimes when the sun is out
You feel great
But if you're feeling faint
You may start to hate someone.
Crying helps to release
A strange belief.

Michael Gowling (12)
Hurworth School - Maths & Computing College

Decisions, Decisions

Chocolate, chocolate,
Which one shall I choose?
White chocolate Buttons,
Or a Milky Bar Choo.

Bounty or Mars bar,
Snickers or Crunchie,
Should I have Minstels
Or could I have Munchies.

Ripple, Maltesers,
Galaxy or Flake,
Dairy Milk, Kit-kat,
A hard decision to make.

Chocolate orange, Bueno,
Caramel, Smarties,
Drifter and Time Out,
Are all good for parties.

So I'll make my decision,
Hard it may be,
And I've decided in the end,
They're all meant for me!

Sabrina Baker (12)
Hurworth School - Maths & Computing College

Cats

When the cats come out to play
their eyes are like light bulbs,
searching for mice.
At daybreak they are playful,
climbing curtains and walls,
sharpening their claws.
Falling, they land on their feet.
Lazy cats at the end of the day,
watch them lie down,
purr and sleep.

Christopher Fitzgerald (12)
Hurworth School - Maths & Computing College

Cats

Little cats with their smooth fur
Listen to how they purr and purr
With their very sharp paws
And their deadly claws
They are very good at climbing
And also good at sighing
Landing on their feet
Which is really neat
Curious cats are nasty and nice
And they are very crafty at hunting mice
Their eyes shine in the light
And they put up a good fight
They are always there for tea
And would love to have a stroke off me.

Ryan Colling (12)
Hurworth School - Maths & Computing College

If I Told You How I Feel

If I told you how I feel
Would you believe me?
And if I told you what I think
Would you still be friends with me?

Ever since I met you
I thought you were really nice,
Now you want me, then you don't
Like I'm a rolling dice.

You'll phone me and ask me to see you,
Then you'll change your mind,
Then next minute you are with me,
And really nice and kind.

Joanne Bartlett (13)
Hurworth School - Maths & Computing College

If I Told You How I Feel

If I told you how I feel,
It would probably make you cry,
For when you were lying in hospital,
I didn't get change to say goodbye.

When the tears that ran down my face,
And the rest of my families,
It makes me so happy to think of the days,
That you and I used to see.

Whenever I felt down,
It wouldn't last for long,
As you made me feel so much better,
With singing a little song.

I am all grown up now,
But this you are not here to see,
In my heart I will remember,
The days when it was just you and me.

Natalie Lawson (12)
Hurworth School - Maths & Computing College

Dragonfly

Dragonfly, dragonfly
On the wall,
Dragonfly, dragonfly
Which way to go?
Dragonfly, dragonfly
Everywhere,
Dragonfly, dragonfly
Don't you dare.
Dragonfly, dragonfly
Do you go left?
Do you go right?
Do you go straight into the light?

Matthew Hall (12)
Hurworth School - Maths & Computing College

Autumn's Here

Everyone's feeling cold
Cold and crisp
Streams are freezing
Autumn's here.

The sun is shining
The leaves are falling
Ice glistens on the ground
Shining all around.

Autumn nights
The fire goes on
Keeping warm
As the snow falls.

Gillian Akers (14)
Hurworth School - Maths & Computing College

My Hamster

My hamster
Nibbles on food,
Twitches his nose,
Runs on his wheel.

My hamster
Plays all day,
Sits up straight,
Looking really cute.

My hamster
Climbs out of his cage,
Into his wheel,
Ready for his next adventure.

Emma Jameson (14)
Hurworth School - Maths & Computing College

My Old Street

I would love to go to my old street again
43 Burnside Road
I had lots of friends
But since I left I have no one.

I miss my friends from my old street
Oh how we would love to meet.
Running round
Singing songs
Having joy and fun.

My friends have probably forgotten me now
I haven't been there for 3 years
I miss them lots, definitely Kaye,
She was the best
And very funny.

Oh how much I wish I never moved
From my old street.

Melissa Wheelhouse (12)
Hurworth School - Maths & Computing College

Caterpillar To Butterfly

Caterpillar, caterpillar
How are you?
Caterpillar, caterpillar
How do you do?
Caterpillar, caterpillar
Go to sleep.
Beautiful butterfly
Spread your wings,
Pretty butterfly
Fly in the wind.

Oliver Wendel (12)
Hurworth School - Maths & Computing College

Sisters

Sometimes you hate them
Sometimes you love them
Sometimes they annoy you
Sometimes they help you.

Pinching your things
Wearing your clothes
Messing up your room
Those are things that annoy you.

Seeing them happy
Watching them play
Telling you that you're the best
This makes you happy.

Those things they do
Crying, laughing, screaming
This makes you realise
It wouldn't be right without them.

Clare Holme (14)
Hurworth School - Maths & Computing College

Shopping

I get some money
and then spend it all,
it goes as quickly as dust
in my local shopping centre.
I go with my mates
and have a laugh,
we shop for
bobbles, make-up and clothes,
we shop till we drop!
Hands full of bags
we travel home on the bus.

Rebecca Boyd (14)
Hurworth School - Maths & Computing College

Why?

I sit at my window,
Looking up at the sky.
I wonder what you think of
And I wonder why.

Why do you hold me when you know it's not right,
Holding me close, holding me tight?
As if you're afraid of letting me go,
As you and me both already know.

Why do you lie to me and not tell the truth,
As if you're afraid of what I might do?
You know me by now and I know you,
Why do you do this, why every day?

Bobbie Sewell (13)
Hurworth School - Maths & Computing College

My Morning

When I wake up in the morning
and the sunlight hurts my eyes
I realise it's just another day
to go and work my life away

As I'm slowly lifting out of bed
and thoughts keep running through my head
I hear my mam shout up at me,
'Hurry up it's 7:23!'

The time has come, I walk to the stop
when the bus is coming down the street
everyone walks over to the path
I hear the stopping of people's feet.

Gemma Baker (13)
Hurworth School - Maths & Computing College

What Am I Doing Here?
(A poem about my first day at primary school)

Here I am in this place,
My eyes agog, a shy grin on my face,
But who are all these girls and boys?
Can I go home and play with my toys?

Oh no it's time for the bell,
I won't like this, I can tell,
Here she comes, looking very fierce,
I'm sure today will end in tears.

Mrs Chaytor tells me where to sit,
I really don't like this one bit.
I want to go, to run away,
I really wish I were at home today.

Now I'm sitting next to a new friend,
Will this day ever end?
It's playtime now, Mrs Chaytor needs her tea
And all I can think is, *I need a wee!*

It's dinnertime now, or so I'm told,
Now I feel a bit more bold.
I think I'll let go of Mrs Fishburn's hand
And have a walk around and survey the land.

The bell has gone again, it's time for home,
I never thought this would come.
My mum's at the gate, she makes a fuss,
Oh my god, I wish I'd come on the bus!

Chris Lapping (14)
Hurworth School - Maths & Computing College

My World

My world is the best, it is far better than all the rest.
I do whatever I want to, I say whatever I want to.

Sometimes I shout, sometimes I scream,
Sometimes I float away into a brilliant dream.
When I dream it is about football, football, football.

My world is the best, it is far better than all the rest.
I play with my friends, I play with my dog,
But when I'm really bored I play with a warthog.

My world is the best, it is far better than all the rest.
I like running round in my playground.
Sometimes I dance, sometimes I take flight,
But sometimes I climb to a really big height.

My world is the best, far better than all the rest.
I play football, me and my friends,
But when we get tired I drive around
In my Mercedes Benz.

James Rickards (12)
Hurworth School - Maths & Computing College

If I Told You How I Feel

If I told you how I feel
Would you feel sad or would you feel bad?

If I told you how I feel
Would you throw a pork pie and hit me in the eye?

If I told you how I feel, would you be happy?
Because every time I look at you it makes me want to smile.

If I told you how I feel and I said that someone was dead,
Would you hit me in the head?

If I told you how I feel
In the end I know you would be happy.

Aaron Yeomans (13)
Hurworth School - Maths & Computing College

If I Told You How I Feel

If I told you how I feel
Would you listen to me more?

All my thoughts and feelings would make you cry
And never let you say bye.

I want you to know that I love you so very much
And I won't bring up the past again.

I would hate it if you went and left me
All by myself.
And when I ever needed you, you were always gone
Without me.

So when I sit in my chair
I cuddle up to my bear
And care about you.

When I look into your sparkly eyes
I see a bear glancing back at me.

That is how I feel!

Colleen Halstead (11)
Hurworth School - Maths & Computing College

I Really Want To Tell You

I really want to tell you how I feel
I really want to tell you I think it's cruel
I really want to tell you they have to beat you
I really want to tell you that's the only way

I really want to tell you that you're lovely
I really want to tell you they have to cook you
I really want to tell you they'll mix you with bacon and cheese
I really want to tell you you'll make a fine omelette

I really want to tell you, that's your life, as an egg.

Martin Black (13)
Hurworth School - Maths & Computing College

Brothers

Big brothers
Little brothers
They're all the same
Not being man enough
To take the blame

Annoying us
Shouting at us
Being rather rude
And thinking they can walk
Around half in the nude!

'Silly you,'
'Stupid you,'
That's all they will say
And ask, 'Do you want McDonald's?'
And then make you pay.

But big brothers
Little brothers
You may think you're cool
But everyone knows
That sisters *rule!*

Francesca Heath (13)
Hurworth School - Maths & Computing College

If I Told You How I Feel

If I told you how I feel
Would you be happy?

If I told you how I feel
Would you be shocked?

Every time I look at you
I regret what I said.

Even when I am really, really down
The thought of you makes me smile.

Armarni Cornforth (13)
Hurworth School - Maths & Computing College

Would You

If I told you how I feel
Would you like me
Or would you not?

If I told you how I feel
Would you be scared
Or would you be cool?

If I told you how I feel
Should I die
Or should I not?

If I told you I was ill
Would you help me
Or would you not?

If I told you how I feel
Should I leave
Or should I not?

Abigail Jones (13)
Hurworth School - Maths & Computing College

If I Told You How I Feel

If I told you how I feel
Would you keep me company?

If I told you how I feel
Would you be my true love?

If I told you how I feel
Would you snuggle up tonight?

If I told you how I feel
Would you go out tonight?

Michael Myers (11)
Hurworth School - Maths & Computing College

Without You

Without you, I am a heart without love
Without you, I feel like a lost dove
Without you, I am a body without a soul
Without you, I can never be whole.

Without you, I'm the world without people
Without you, I will be no more
Without you, there is no point in living
Without you, I will not be me
So please stay, don't set me free.

Don't let me be without you
Don't let me be alone
Don't let me be taken away from my home
Don't change me from being me!

Joanne Haywood (13)
Hurworth School - Maths & Computing College

The Cheetah

A cheetah, wild in his terror
runs around like a stampeding elephant.
his relation, the tiger, even more fierce than him,
roaming around as if it's a king.

His sleek performance
makes him a dangerous predator
looking around secretly,
spying on his prey.

He finally catches the animal
and takes it home to feed,
him and his cheetah family
feasting on meat.

Cameron Dulston (14)
Hurworth School - Maths & Computing College

If I Told You How I Feel

If I told you how I feel
Would you be angry
Or would you still love me?

If I told you how I feel
Would you leave me
Or would you miss me?

If I told you how I feel
Would you be happy
Or would you not believe me?

If I told you how I feel
Would you care for me
Or would you run away?

If I told you that I was dying
Would you help me
Or would you kill me?

If I told you that I was sick
Would you take care of me
Or would you leave me alone?

If I was left outside alone
Would you take me home
Or would you leave me there?

Amy Wilson (13)
Hurworth School - Maths & Computing College

In Space No One Can Hear You Scream

Running, running, past the bridge of an outdated ship,
Running, running, past a window of darkness.
Behind, the creature follows, tearing up everything in its way,
Running, running, through the closing doors as the sirens sound.
Under the door, under the door, in front of the door,
As the hydraulic lock locks with a clang.
In space no one can hear you scream.

Adrian Balmer (12)
Hurworth School - Maths & Computing College

The Footie Match

Football is my favourite game
I play it every day
Bag a hat-trick in the net
And hey we're on our way
To victory, to victory.

        Right, it's a goal kick
        It's past the midfield
        Fowler picks his important spot
        Weh, hey it's four on the trot
        Victory, oh victory!

The ball is driven up the field
Fowler used his amazing speed
He goes to the left
He goes to the right
Then strikes the ball with all his might
The keeper pounces but he doesn't succeed
Fowler thanks his amazing speed.

Sean Fowler (13)
Hurworth School - Maths & Computing College

If I Told You How I Feel

If I told you how I feel would you jump for joy
Or cry like a little boy?
No one knows how I feel except for my heart
Which makes me feel the way I feel
Like a mouse in a field which has no cares in the world.
Am I happy, am I sad?
I don't know because I am glad.
The way I feel playing in this field
Because I have told you how I feel.

Nathan Bickerton (11)
Hurworth School - Maths & Computing College

If I Told You How I Feel

If I told you how I feel
Just look me in the eye
Then you'll see my gorgeous smile
And then I'll tell you why.

You're beautiful, you're calm
You never tell a lie
You always get me lots of stuff.

You're funny, you're kind
You always read my mind
I'll tell you a lot of good secrets that you will tell no one.

You're loving, you're caring
You take me lots of places for a laugh
And you're always game for a laugh.

You'll always love me as much as you can.

Kelly Ward (11)
Hurworth School - Maths & Computing College

Hard To Believe

Hard to believe I am a movie star
Hard to believe I can jump very far
Hard to believe I can visit the moon
Hard to believe I can sing in tune
Hard to believe I like runner beans
Hard to believe I've got a song in the charts
Hard to believe I am very smart
Easy to believe I'm lying in my bed
Making this all up in my head.

Lily Hamilton (12)
Hurworth School - Maths & Computing College

My Mum

My Mum is so lazy
She never gets out of bed
She sleeps like a dormouse
And only eats bread

She sits and watches telly
With her big fat belly
She never stops talking
And is never walking

When she drives her car
She's like a mad dog
And she loves White Star
But she is a bed hog

When we go to town
She always buys loads
Her favourite colour is brown
And she can't stand toads

Her bedroom is a tip
You would think it was a skip
Her favourite programme is Corrie
And she never says sorry

So here's a poem for you
We know not all of it is true
But here's to the laziest mum.

Lauren Burton (12)
Hurworth School - Maths & Computing College

I Got Your Back

I got your back
You got mine
I'll help you out
Anytime.

To see you hurt
To see you cry
Makes me weep
And wanna die.

And if you agree
To never fight
It wouldn't matter
Who's wrong or right.

If a broken heart
Needs to mend
I'll be there
To the end.

If you are wet
From drops of tears
Don't you worry
Let go of your fears.

Hand in hand
Love is sent
We'll be friends
Till the end.

Craig Robinson (12)
Hurworth School - Maths & Computing College

The Night Out

Out on the town for a good night out
Me and my friends, we all shout
So many people in the crowd
Oh so loud! Oh so loud!
Then comes an awful sound
Someone has fallen to the ground
In a beam of light
We see a fight
Headlights glare
I'm scared
So home again
It's starting to rain
It will be a long time
Before I go there again.

Fiona Hamilton (12)
Hurworth School - Maths & Computing College

Wild Horses

Horses are galloping, running around,
The sun is setting,
To the peaceful sound.
The birds are tweeting
The horses are seeking,
For food they search
And grass they churn.
The darkness is emerging
And midges are in flight.
They huddle together
Throughout the misty night.

Victoria Osborne (12)
Hurworth School - Maths & Computing College

My Friends And I

My friends and I
Talk all day
We tell stories
Happy and sad

Good friends like us
We're friends forever
The longer it lasts
The more fun it will be.

Ashleigh Hall (12)
Hurworth School - Maths & Computing College

Smoking

If I told you how I feel
Your skin would crack and peel
Your face would sag like a bag
I never should have smoked that fag

I only smoked a drag
A rolled up paper bag
If you knew how I felt
You would hit me with a belt.

Robert Forster (13)
Hurworth School - Maths & Computing College

The Little Cat

There was a little cat
Who was very, very fat
She tried catching a mouse
That ran into the house
And ran into my room
It crawled into my boot
When I went to put my boot on
It gave me a fright.

Lesley Medland (12)
Hurworth School - Maths & Computing College

The School Bus

Day after day
I am on the school bus
Walk down the street
Without a fuss

I get to the bus stop
Wait for a while
I hop on the bus
And I don't see you smile

The journey is quiet
No not a sound
I look out the window
I can see all around

I see fields
That hold cows
I see farmers in tractors
Pulling their ploughs

We pass through villages
I see people walking
As I sit on the bus
No one is talking

Then the odd cough
Here and there
When anyone talks
All they get is a stare

Finally we arrive at school
We pull in the school gate
I get off the bus
And again we are late!

Ben Harper (13)
Hurworth School - Maths & Computing College

The Big, Bad Boy!

His head is spiky
So he picks on Mickey
He is yellow
And thinks he is the fellow

He is naughty
He thinks he is cool
He likes guns
And he hates school

Because he is naughty
He thinks he rules
Because he is a prankster
He is not cool

He is popular at school
And a bit of a bully
People think he is cool
But he is big and he drools

He shoots pigeons
He shoots rabbits
He stuffs them
Then displays them

He kills foxes
And local pheasants
Then stuffs them
Which isn't very pleasant

He's a bad boy
Oh no a bad boy
Oh such a very
Big, bad boy.

Joanna Dinsdale (14)
Hurworth School - Maths & Computing College

Holiday Blues

My holiday to Florida was meant to be great,
but hurricane Francis took it away,
until a lady rang us with some great news,
that we could go somewhere else to admire the views.

We chose to go to Sa Coma, a destination in Spain,
which took two hours on a huge blue plane.
When we got there it was one in the morning,
so everything seemed to be quite boring.

The next day came and we played in the pool,
my dad went on stage and looked a fool.
The day soon came when we had to say bye,
I even had a tear in my eye,
because what started off as a holiday from Hell,
ended up going very, very well.

Becky Mullett (13)
Hurworth School - Maths & Computing College

Feelings

Many people have feelings
Many people don't
Some say it's special
But others don't
But then again . . .
What's the point in hating each other
When we could live happily
With no war, fighting, hatred or anything bad
We could live happily, peacefully, quietly
All of this instead.

Rachel Dauber (13)
Hurworth School - Maths & Computing College

The Hounds

Over the fields and into the valley
The hounds got the scent of a hare
Down the slope and over the stream
The hounds got the scent of a hare.

Up on the moors and through the heather
The hounds got the scent of a hare
Through the woods and into the marsh
The hounds got the scent of a hare.

Along the hedge line and through the grass
The hounds got the scent of a hare
Over the wall and under the fence
The hounds got the scent of a hare.

The hare wasn't seen again!

Carl Jameson (13)
Hurworth School - Maths & Computing College

I Wish

I wish I could hold you now
I wish I could touch you now
I wish I could talk to you
Be with you somehow
I know you're in a better place
I know I can't see your face
I know you're smiling down on me
Saying everything's OK
Wishing I had a 'thug' life
See you again someday
I wish, I wish, I wish
I wish, I wish, I wish.

Catherine Morton (14)
Hurworth School - Maths & Computing College

Heaven Or Hell?

Where will you go?
Can you go so low,
Or up high,
Where the angels fly?
Heaven is full of wonderful things,
Glitter and angels' wings.
Rainbows and light,
While in Hell it's all fright.
Devils and horns,
And demons' thorns.
Smoke and fire,
And there's always a lair.
So where will you end up?
You can't go into the future and look.
So it all depends on how you act on Earth,
All starting from birth.

Nichola Bateman (13)
Hurworth School - Maths & Computing College

So Much Fun

Playing in the sea
Is so much fun
Splashing in the waves
Lying in the sun
Eating ice cream
Is so much fun
Watching donkeys having a lie down
Building sandcastles
Is so much fun
Watching crabs nibbling at your toes.

Robyn Simpson (13)
Hurworth School - Maths & Computing College

Heaven

Above the fluffy white clouds
A winter wonderland
Angels sing and dance
Their white robes flowing
Along with their golden curls
Their white feathery wings
And golden halos
For this is a better place
To come forever more
Sunshine and white cloud
Peace and protection
No more war
Cultures together as friends
For this is what the world should be like.

Clare Eddy (13)
Hurworth School - Maths & Computing College

War

If you want to fight
That's fine by me
You can lose men's lives
That's fine by me
Blow things up
Whatever you want
Another British life wasted
To the gun of another man
Just remember this
When I grow up
I won't fight for you.

Tom Flynn (13)
Hurworth School - Maths & Computing College

If I Told You How I Feel

If I told you how I feel,
Would you be there for me?
Would you be my friend,
Would you care for me?

You're caring, you're funny
You're always up for a laugh.

If I told you how I feel,
Could I tell you secrets?
Would you tell a peep,
Could I look up to you?

You're caring, you're funny
You're always up for a laugh.

Chloë Carlton (11)
Hurworth School - Maths & Computing College

Music

When we listen to music
We can all start to smile
And when we get on the dance floor
We suddenly start to dance
But the great thing about music
Is that there is a song for your every mood
And no matter how bad you feel
It can always make you smile
So get down on the dance floor
And start to move!

Beth Frankland (13)
Hurworth School - Maths & Computing College

War

Hitler will send no warning
always carry your gas mask
he wants to rule us
he shall not rule us.

War is pain
war is heartache
war is crazy
war has begun.

People killing
people dying
almost everyone crying
plus children dying.

Joshua Crane (13)
Hurworth School - Maths & Computing College

Drugs

That little pill, that little pill
Have you given up or just don't care?
Or did you do it for a dare?
Now you can't stop and just want more
So get help and open up the door
Because otherwise you will lose the pace
To carry on the human race
So pick yourself up and carry on
Because soon you will be having fun
That little pill, that little pill.

Richard Minto (13)
Hurworth School - Maths & Computing College

I Wish!

If I wish upon a star
Would all of my dreams come true?
Would you ever think of me
The way I think of you?
Would you notice me standing here
Or would you look straight through?
Because my love for you is getting greater
If only you ever knew!

Clare Rudd (13)
Hurworth School - Maths & Computing College

Sunset

The soft sand blows beneath my feet,
The sky's covered with a dark blue sheet,
Small shining stars are twinkling high,
As I watch the midnight sky.

An orange shape,
Starts to take shape,
A fist of wind blows on my face,
The sunset is an amazing case.

Small, dark boats are sailing past,
Over shadows the sun has cast.

Twinkling stars start to form,
The tide has come slowly in,
The sun is in the shape of a dome,
Sunset.

Danielle Sharkey (11)
Lord Lawson Of Beamish School

The Third Age

The war is here,
The battle has come,
Swords are drawn,
Arrows are flung.

One white wall,
To protect us all,
The horns of evil,
Frighten the feeble.

An alliance has failed,
Help did not come,
Only one army stands,
And they stand alone.

The armour clanks,
My men fear death,
Rocks fall on us,
Trebuchets are released like angry wolves.

The doors have been breached,
Orcs and trolls file in like water,
This is the end,
The end has come.

Wait! Green cloaks and horses,
The Rohirrim have come,
Elves and men side by side once more,
We shall shed blood together this night.

Craig Atherton (13)
Lord Lawson Of Beamish School

The Funny Story Of Isaac Newton

Many years ago,
Centuries I would say,
A boy called Isaac Newton was born,
And is still remembered today.

He was a normal kid,
Although you know, a bit of a swat,
He was the best at science,
He knew every answer, the lot!

Later in life, he became a brainy scientist,
And worked all day and night,
And then one very special day,
He had a really nasty fright.

Plop! The apple landed on his head.
'Ouch!' he cried, 'oh deary me!'
He sat down and had a think,
This is *gravity!*

So he discovered gravity and a lot of other stuff too,
'He is so intelligent,' everyone said,
'A genius.' But it is a great shame because
He is dead.

Naomi Lea (11)
Lord Lawson Of Beamish School

The Ghost

It hovers across the marble floor,
Slowly approaching the open door.
Gradually it falls to the ground,
So slow, so quiet, without making a sound.

It strives to end its life of pain,
A task which is definitely carried out in vain.

Alex Stoker (13)
Lord Lawson Of Beamish School

Eternal Travelling
(Based on Stephen King's short story 'The Jaunt')

Jaunting . . .
Destroying all known laws of physics,
Sleeping through the trip,
Distorting time and space.
But if you try it awake . . .
It's longer than you think.

Jaunting . . .
You arrive at your destination,
In less time than you thought,
But there's always one that wonders,
What if you try it awake?
It's longer than they think.

Jaunting . . .
So then they hold their breath,
When the gas is given to them,
Pushed through the portal,
Trying it awake . . .
But it's longer than they think.

Jaunting . . .
Now they have realised,
Jaunting takes less than a second physically,
But it's an eternity mentally!
They tried it awake . . .
And it was longer than they did think!

Jaunting . . .
Like moss creeping down a mountainside,
The passage of time takes an eternity to end.
Glassy eyes and a frazzled brain,
Try it awake and you'll soon die . . .
Because it's longer than anyone thinks.

Daniel Norton (13)
Lord Lawson Of Beamish School

Dreams

I start in the wild, wild west,
I am wearing a sheriff's crest,
I jump on a fast horse,
But it runs off course.
Bam! Bam! Bam!
I wake up at my school,
The air is wet and cool,
I see the scary robot teacher,
But I'm never going to reach her.
Bam! Bam! Bam!
I find myself in a graveyard,
I fall over the rocks, the grass is hard,
Lightning strikes down,
A zombie rises from the ground a clown.
Bam! Bam! Bam!
I wake up in a field of magic,
A tiny dog comes up to me with an unusual gadget,
The sun is shining in my eye,
I smell a distant smell of pie.
Bam! Bam! Bam!
I wake up, am I up or really dreaming?
I feel my face, it's peeling,
I hear a squawking voice shout up the stairs,
I fall over my dressing table's chair,
As I walk to the stairs,
I start rising into the air,
I receive a strange feeling,
As I float up to the ceiling,
I bark like a pup,
I then finally wake up!

Stacey Davidson (11)
Lord Lawson Of Beamish School

Cars, Lots Of Cars

Cars, cars, they make you think
Going fast your heart sinks
Skinny ones, fat ones, small ones - fast
You always want the feeling to last.

Noise, alloys, spoilers and roof scoops
Often the focus of a new supe up!
Big exhausts and many more
Stuff on cars you have to adore.

New cars looked at by many
Posh ones such as Bentley
Most are practicals driven by others
Little silly ones driven by mothers.

Loads of cars on the roads
Big huge trucks carrying loads
Boy racers in the night
As the engines roar, it's a speed fight.

As all the cars turn the bend
The power will come to an end
What vehicle will you choose?
Pick a good one so you don't lose!

Alex Bills (12)
Lord Lawson Of Beamish School

Feelings

I have so many feelings,
I just can't hide,
I try to lock them down deep inside.
All my anger, all my hope,
Sometimes I wonder if I can cope.
There's nowhere to run, nowhere to hide,
My feelings take over in the night.
I lie awake unable to dream,
It's like a nightmare,
I just want to wake and scream.

Christina Bailey (13)
Lord Lawson Of Beamish School

Hallowe'en

Hallowe'en is a spooky night
The full moon shines big and bright
Kids get dressed up as black cats
Or witches with pointed hats
Devils all dressed in red
Walking down the street with a sword through their head
Skeletons with spider webs in-between their bones
A zombie walks by with grunts and groans
A vampire with blood-drenched fangs
From his neck his head hangs
Mummies wrapped in toilet roll
Around the street floats a lost soul
A big, dead, scary ghost
Frightened everyone the most
Pumpkins carved with scary faces
Headless knights walk by with maces
All these monsters knocking on doors
Some with sharp pointed claws
They are greeted with a bag of candy
Which later will come in handy
Then they get home and take their masks off
And the candy they do scoff
Chocolate bars and candy sticks
Lollipops everyone licks
Jelly beans and bubblegum
Won't be enough to fill their tum
Now the sweets are all gone
Nothing left for anyone
Remember the time when the full moon shone
And everyone was having fun?

Kathryn Simm (12)
Lord Lawson Of Beamish School

All Alone

All alone, by myself
Don't know where to go
This way and that way
All my friends, gone
Got no one to play with
Help, help I'm trapped
In my room all alone
No one there to help me
No one there to guide me
A knock on the door
And someone comes in
Who I do not know
I scream and I shout, 'Let me out, let me out!'
But the door slams shut
Like a little old hut
I go to sleep but I weep and I weep
And never wake again.

Louise Pearson (11)
Lord Lawson Of Beamish School

Untitled

The moon goes over in the dead of night
The show's in the daylight
Eminem always swears and curses
But still writes very good verses
A bird glides through the air
They fly over here and fly over there
A river flows through calmly
Like wind blowing a palm tree
War will break our world down
And the whole world will wear a frown.

Stuart Ranson (11)
Lord Lawson Of Beamish School

Parties!

Parties are great, parties are fun,
It's so much better when you're playing in the sun.
Spending time with one another,
But definitely not your little brother.

No boys allowed, is the sign on the door,
Lots of food being spilt on the floor.
Having fun is what it's all about,
Making lots of noise as we shout.

Lots of people and lots of chat,
Having a good time in my brand new flat.
Music can be heard all around,
As we party through the night, whilst making lots of sound.

Parties are great, parties are fun.
They're also great when you're playing in the sun.
Spending time with one another,
But definitely not your little brother.

Ellen Ridley (11)
Lord Lawson Of Beamish School

My Little Sister

I am happy I have a sister as great as you,
You make me smile and laugh until the day is through,
You help me when I am sad, you're fab to me,
And as long as we're together happy I will be.

I enjoy it when I play as you're like a best friend,
We will fall out and fight but it's never the end,
I love it when we're together, no matter what the weather,
We'll always be together because I love you such a lot.

I always pick you up after school,
You think it's really very cool,
But sometimes when you want to play,
I have to say, 'Go away,' because homework usually comes my way.

Abigail Smith (12)
Lord Lawson Of Beamish School

Things That Go Bump In The Night

This Hallowe'en was by far the best
Scary mind but better than the rest
I was getting ready, make-up and all
When all of a sudden there was a knock on the door
I jumped downstairs, my cape in the air
So excited to see who was there . . .

It was my mates you see, the troublesome lot
So off we went with our plan intact
There's a man that lives next to Mr Slight
There's a rumour going around that he murders at night
We had to find out so we went to his house
Spooky lanterns everywhere, a cat chasing a mouse.

My bones got the chills, I got such a fright
There was a long, hollow screech and out went the lights
A black shadow beckoned, groaning in pain
'It's him,' Alice screamed, 'he's murdered again!'
Without looking back we whimpered and scarpered
All I could think about was a bloodstained carpet.

At nine o'clock there was a knock on the door
It was him, I almost fainted on the floor
'I didn't mean to scare you, here's some candy for free
I fell over, there was a powercut you see'
'Thank you,' I said, 'but what was with the groan?'
'My cat, I'm sorry, I tripped over her, it made me fall.'

That explained a lot, I thought to myself
That's the last time I listen to anyone else
'A man that murders,' it was all a silly story
At least I hope so, they make my skin go creepy-crawly.

Louise Taylor (11)
Lord Lawson Of Beamish School

My Walking Seal

My walking seal,
Soft and brown,
Nerves of steel,
Deserves a crown.

My walking seal,
Never goes astray,
Stays at my heel,
Until the end of the day.

My walking seal,
Like the settee,
Eats orange peel,
And drops bits on me.

My walking seal,
Silky and snappy,
Makes me feel
Oh so happy.

My walking seal,
So full of fun,
He's a real hot deal,
As hot as the sun.

My walking seal,
His name rhymes with rake,
He can eat big meals,
But he isn't a snake.

My walking seal,
Clean and fresh,
Could make a wheel,
Out of mesh.

My walking seal,
Is so clever,
He doesn't squeal,
He is mine forever.

My walking seal,
Have you guessed yet?
My walking seal,
Is the family pet.

Becci Smith (12)
Lord Lawson Of Beamish School

The Room

The man walked into a room,
He waited for hours but for nothing,
He waited not knowing, to seek his doom.

A cloaked figure with hair hanging down,
Spotted the man in the room,
He sneaked in silence all around.

The man in the room was unaware,
That a man was coming,
Coming up the stair.

The lights went out,
The man was shocked,
It was danger without a doubt.

Nowhere to run, nowhere to hide,
He wasn't alone,
In for a bumpy ride.

The sound of a bullet flying,
A screaming man,
The scream of dying.

Tabitha Dickinson (11)
Lord Lawson Of Beamish School

The Fight

In a dark street, on a dark night,
Two young men had a gory fight,
Everyone saw it when they came,
But still, nobody knows who was to blame.

Ben was the first to strike,
He had a broken bottle and a Stanley knife,
He slashed Brett across the arm,
Which made him cower and shriek in pain.

Brett tried to fight but then his legs turned weak,
His life, he thought, was turning bleak,
Ben suddenly got into his car,
Then drove into Brett, which made him fly far.

Ben made an escape when he saw the police come,
The chances of Brett surviving looked glum,
The police chased Ben in a mad dash,
But he was persistent and went too fast.

Ben ran from his car at Westhill Road,
And rushed into a deserted abode,
The police finally cornered him in a small room,
But then everyone heard a majestic boom!

Ben had been shot in the chest,
Brett came in with a gun and said, 'Now we know who's the best!'

Daniel Harrison (11)
Lord Lawson Of Beamish School

Crunch

The snail, with his spirally shell
Squelches across the garden
Then . . .
Crunch!
The snail is dead.

Katherine Saunders (11)
Lord Lawson Of Beamish School

Seasons

Leaves, leaves falling down
Falling down in their colourful gown.

Oak leaves, yew leaves
Sycamore too
In the spring they start anew.

All of a sudden
The trees are bare
Like a graveyard
In a nightmare.

Then comes the snow
The wind, the rain
The hailstones cause increasing pain.

Then the spring
Returns again
Winter coming
And leaving in vain.

The leaves return
On the trees
And the birds
Fly with bees.

Long summer nights
Follow that
And the night
Is silent as a bat.

And autumn returns
With its ferns
Evergreens and its leaves.

Then the process starts again
With wind, sun and then the rain.

Alex Richings (13)
Lord Lawson Of Beamish School

The Writer Of This Poem
(Based on 'The Writer Of This Poem' by Roger McGough)

The writer of this poem is
As fine as a flower,
As pretty as a pig,
As sly as a snake.

The writer of this poem is
As sweet as sugar,
As happy as a hippo,
As busy as a bee.

The writer of this poem is
As tall as a tower,
As forgetful as a fish,
As mad as a monkey.

The writer of this poem is never to be found,
As the writer of this poem is not around.

Alison Waltham (11)
Lord Lawson Of Beamish School

Watch Them Grow

Watch them grow to tall from low,
Watch their voice break as they eat their twelfth birthday cake.

Watch their old friends fade away,
As they grow bigger every day.

Watch them finish their old school,
Watch them try to be cool.

Watch them move out and buy a car,
Watch them have kids with sweets in a jar.

Watch their hair turn really grey,
Until their very last day . . .

Sean Mullen (11)
Lord Lawson Of Beamish School

Derby

Man United v Man City,
We all felt a little pity,
For City who had their second team,
For United who were in gleam.

Dunn confessed to his injured calf,
And on came their brilliant centre half,
At half-time they all went in,
And there was Fergie with a grin.

Then Van Nistelroy got injured too,
And all their fans started to boo,
On came the brilliant Nicky Butt,
With his excellent right foot.

Man U was the first to score,
And all their fans started to roar,
All of City's heads went down,
And there was Keegan with a frown.
The final whistle blows - 1-0!

Dean Stewart (11)
Lord Lawson Of Beamish School

English

English comes in different sorts,
Verbs and words, nouns and phrases,
Some are easy, some are hard,
And some are always on the board.

English comes in different sorts,
Suffix and prefix, and naughty boys,
Girls are quiet, boys are bad
And some of us have to stand outside.

Emma McCullen (12)
Lord Lawson Of Beamish School

Bogies!

I love bogies
They are so yummy
They wriggle and squiggle
And squirm in my tummy

Sometimes they're yellow
Sometimes they're green
Sometimes they're fat
Sometimes they're lean

You can get them with fish
And some with horseradish
Sometimes it can be a real treat
On dinner with potatoes and meat

Of course my favourite of all
Is picking one that's really tall
Then aiming the target spot
And flicking it into a baby's cot!

Alex Turnbull (11)
Lord Lawson Of Beamish School

Fireworks

When they fire into the air,
It makes me stare.
When the capsule explodes,
Lots of colours come out in loads.
When the fire burns bright,
I see it in my sight.
And the fireworks go bang,
On the night Guy Fawkes sang.

It is the time of day,
When we pull out the tray.
I see a rocket in a packet,
Which will soon make a racket.
Fireworks, fireworks lighting up the sky,
And we hope the end is not nigh.

Phillip McKenna (12)
Lord Lawson Of Beamish School

The Snake

The sun blazes through the trees overhead,
The long, slinky snake rising from his bed,
A creature, small scuttles by.

The mouse gives a loud, screeching cry,
The snake lies low in the undergrowth,
First sign of the prey and off he goes.

The mile-long creature races past,
But sadly the mouse is not as fast,
Skin snagging on thorn it wanders,
Close behind comes the anaconda!

The sky turns black,
Thunder claps,
Snake jaws snap.

Soon the timid mouse is gone,
Many more creatures pass,
But the beast doesn't follow,
For he has had his feast.

Charlotte Maughan (12)
Lord Lawson Of Beamish School

Winter

The summer has gone and winter came
All the children are inside playing their games
Watching the snow drift ever so lightly
And the star shining oh so brightly
There's no children playing in the street
As the workers come home with clumps of snow on their feet
The gleaming ice on the path
The sky is ever so black
As I look out of my window
The world is just a fog
All I can see is, what is close to me
My hand, window and *snow!*

Alison Peel (12)
Lord Lawson Of Beamish School

Europe - A Series Of Comical Limericks

There once was a man from Belarus,
Who thought he was the god Zeus,
He tried to throw lightning,
The result was quite frightening,
And you can't say he ran out of juice.

There once was a man from Liechtenstein,
Who wanted to stand in a line,
He queued up at Dover,
Got trampled all over,
And ended up snapping his spine.

There once was a man from Spain,
Who was allergic to rain,
He went out with no coat,
Ended up in a moat,
And was found howling in pain.

There once was a man from France,
Who always wore steel underpants,
He said, 'Once I sinned,
And sat on a pin,
And I'll never again take a chance.'

There once was a man who was Russian,
Who was very good at pushin',
Somewhere where he was new,
He pushed right through the queue,
Just to buy himself a cushion.

There once was a man from Germany,
Who wanted to eat his tea,
He decided to have more,
Until he reached his front door,
And found he'd lost his key.

Jonathan Lloyd (11)
Lord Lawson Of Beamish School

My Holiday

In August, summer 2003,
We went on holiday, my family and me.
We were just getting ready when we couldn't find the dosh,
We were running around in a bit of a rush.
Guess who found it and saved the day?
Me, so now we can pay.
Car journeys are always a bore,
And they make everyone apart from the driver snore.
When we arrived at the place we were staying,
It is fantastic, we were all saying.
The food on the plate,
Was absolutely great.
We went on a boat up and down the lake,
It took ages for goodness sake.
The next day we went to Coniston, it was windy and raining,
My mum's umbrella was really straining.
Then we went for the weekly quiz,
And guess which team were the whiz.
We won the prize,
A bottle of wine that was quite a size.
That's not fair, it made me think,
Because I can't drink.
Even though I had some,
Without telling my mum.
On the final day we went to a wildlife park,
And some of the animals were out of their cages which was
                                                                                   a bit of a lark.
Finally we went back home and I said,
'It's nice to sleep in your own comfy bed!'

Andrew McCarton (11)
Lord Lawson Of Beamish School

Changing Seasons

Spring is the start of a new year,
Everyone takes off their warm winter fur,
The flowers bloom very bright,
The sun shining in my sight,
The butterflies come out and fly,
The birds singing in the sky.

Summer comes full of sun,
Playing on the beach, having fun,
Splashing around in the pool,
On holiday, keeping cool,
Getting a bit of sun, sea and sand,
Staying in hotels that look very grand.

Autumn arrives with wind and rain,
Blustery winds will not tame,
Crispy leaves beneath my feet,
Trees swaying slightly in the street,
Orange leaves float down to the ground,
Float down to the ground without a sound.

Winter soon comes along with snow,
And a visit from Santa - ho, ho, ho!
Frosty ice and snowy roads,
People coming down with nasty colds,
Snowflakes in the air glitter and shimmer,
As the nights get dimmer and dimmer.

Alicia Forster (11)
Lord Lawson Of Beamish School

Chocolate

A creamy tingle follows every bite,
Like tangy shocks fizzing around your mouth,
That's why we love chocolate - always right . . .
All round the world, from the north to the south,
The warm aroma and the gorgeous smell,
The happy shiver as soon as you buy . . .
The heat, the warming, you know it so well,
You wait, you're longing, you're desperate to try.
It comes in boxes, small packets and bars,
So snug in its wrapping - bright and so crisp,
It calls from sweet shops, both near and afar,
The call of a Mars and the Cadbury's Wispa,
The rush, the taste when you've just licked it,
You know, you're alive - yes, you're addicted.

'Mmm . . . '

Abby Glass (13)
Polam Hall School

A Mother's Sonnet On Mobile Phones

Today most people have a mobile 'thing'
To text and talk at every time of day
To harass us with their polyphonic ring
To pose and model, always on display
Lots now have cameras, no reason why
Just useless gadgets, overpriced and loud
Just fashion toys, a way to make us buy
The latest version to show to the crowd
But this new fashion doesn't stop with phones
People are judged by all the clothes they wear
What they earn and what kind of car they own
This money judgement simply isn't fair
Why is the world so obsessed with style?
To work that out will take us quite a while.

Jade Clark (14)
Polam Hall School

Summer

The end of summer always comes too soon
And then the leaves they wither and they fall
The leaves, a carpet spread across a room
The trees are bare but still they stand so tall
The smell of the grass when it has just been mown
The sun glares down at all the passers by
The rain has come and now the summer's gone
Though not all's bad when the summer goes by
The snow will fall and then turn into ice
The children get wrapped up and go to play
The views through all the windows can't be priced
Then go to your warm house from the cold day
The summer may have gone, the winter's here
But warmth will soon come back - next summer's near!

Jessica Crawford (13)
Polam Hall School

Summer Sonnet

The end of summer always comes too soon,
The end of doing what you want has come.
The end of flowers always being in bloom,
Of everyone being joyful, all is done.
The farmers gather harvests - wheat and corn,
The last of summer's beauty, golden skies,
All waits to be refreshed, to be reborn,
While everything on Earth just slowly dies.
But autumn brings new colours to delight,
Collecting conkers, catching falling leaves,
And winter closes in to make day night,
Cold weather, mists, frost, ice and stormy seas.
So don't just sit inside and count the days,
The holidays will end, so go and play!

Lucinda Bailey Thompson (14)
Polam Hall School

Myself

You look in my eyes, you see a smile
Do you think that you see into my soul?
This is a side of me once in a while
It's every part of me which makes me whole
I look up at the ever changing sky
And see its constant movement through the day
My moods are just like that - I wonder why
Nobody seems to see that I'm that way
Although I'm ever changing like the moon
The memories inside will always stay
But even if I leave this Earth too soon
Would it pass by as if a normal day?
They maybe see some things I cannot see
Is all the world just laughing back at me?

Rebecca Harrison (13)
Polam Hall School

Sheep

As new day dawns we sheep are very tense
As underneath the sycamore we meet.
We sidle alongside the barbed wire fence
And there's a cattle grid to trap our feet.
But not being quite as stupid as they think,
We use our brains and come up with a plan.
We run up to the grid and on the brink
We tuck our legs and roll the best we can.
The villagers all stare as we arrive,
A sheep attack is not what they expect.
But as we start to eat, they start to drive
Us back to our field, they don't suspect
That sheep aren't always just what sheep might seem,
Under our coats, we've proved that we can dream.

Lucy Downes (13)
Polam Hall School

Who Am I?

When I look at myself, what do I see?
I see myself as bitter, weak and cold,
I can't remember who I used to be,
I'm fifty now, is that so very old?
When I was younger, life seemed good and true,
I ran and danced and felt completely free,
But now what other things are there to do?
What other things are there for me to be?
I think from time to time I'll go away,
And travel round the world before I'm dead,
But then I feel that I should really stay,
I know they wouldn't happen like I've read,
Am I to wake and see the Northern Lights?
I'm not sure yet but one day I just might!

Polly Enevoldson (13)
Polam Hall School

My Mother's Sonnet

My mother thinks that she could be a star,
She thinks the weekly shopping is a race.
She thinks she could go racing in her car,
A Skoda, which she drives with speed not grace.
When cooking she thinks she is Delia Smith,
Out shopping she thinks that she is Giselle.
She thinks it's cool to say someone's 'a dish',
But if my friends dare to say, 'What the hell!'
But if Mum wasn't here, what would I do?
I need her to help me through every day
When I need help it's Mum that I turn to.
When other people leave, Mum always stays.
My life just wouldn't be my life if I
Didn't have my mum standing by my side.

Lydia Burnside-Hughes (13)
Polam Hall School

A Frog's Tale

The tiny tadpoles wriggling in the pond
They're swimming in and out through rocks and leaves
And sticking fast to form their jelly bond
They come up every now and then to breathe
Their long and slimy tails splash side to side
Their black and beady eyes shift to and fro
They creep in crevices to try to hide
And sneak and crawl to try to keep down low
Now when these tadpoles change into a frog
They come from water onto solid ground
They hop and leap and slide from log to log
And bathe in pools as if they were half-drowned.

They may well change and start to breathe the air,
But I still think they're horrid - I don't care!

Dominique Forrest (13)
Polam Hall School

Life

Whenever life is good to me,
I know that something bad will spoil it.
Sun will shine but then it rains,
It pours and then it snows,
So nothing good will stay, or will be mine.
If ever I'm invited to a rave,
You bet, I'll always get a massive zit.
No matter how I try to keep being brave,
It gets too much and I'm so sick of it.
I wish my problems would just fly away,
And life would start to be more fair to me.
'Just hold your head up high,' that's what I say,
There's no way you can ever be set free.
So this is what I'm saying in my verse,
Life may be boring, then it just gets worse.

Hannah Dent Noble (14)
Polam Hall School

When I Look At Myself

When I look at myself what do I see?
Of course I see a girl, but then also
I see myself just looking back at me.
I look again before I turn to go
And nothing changes; this is still my hair,
My bitten nails and my unpierced nose,
Mascaraed eyelashes, my cold, hard stare,
The scuffed, old trainers and my casual clothes.
But when I look more closely then I find
There's something else that I cannot control,
A personality that was behind.
It's written in my mind and in my soul,
So never judge a person until you
Have challenged what it is you thought you knew.

Kate Sayer (13)
Polam Hall School

Summer

Why do I like the summer quiet so much?
The trips, the seaside, ice cream everywhere,
The picnics on the grass, the sun's warm touch,
The freedom and the lovely food to share.
Just lying in my garden makes me brown,
With ice-cool drinks and shades and paper plates.
I love a water fight to cool me down,
A barbecue with family and mates,
But maybe it's because there is no school,
For eight whole weeks, no lessons, no thinking.
To be on holiday is really cool,
Listening to music, having a sing.
I think that this must really be the reason,
That summer's always my favourite season.

Lucy Watson (13)
Polam Hall School

Brussel Sprouts

'Eat up your sprouts! Don't push them to one side!'
All mums around the world say to their kids.
I can't help thinking I should run and hide,
I mean, who made them? I will kill who did!
Reminding me of curled up greenish slugs,
Like cabbages all shrunken in the wash.
They're smelly little blighters, full of bugs,
They're nothing special, no, they're nothing posh.
At Christmas which is my favourite time,
The sprouts have taken over Christmas tea,
That's why I've written out this little rhyme.
I hope that now I've really made you see,
Nutritious as these sprouts may seem to you,
We all should go and flush them down the loo.

Vicki Lauren Pugh (13)
Polam Hall School

My Parents

My parents always think that they are right,
They never listen to my point of view,
Determined to make me see in their light,
Though I am sick of being told what to do.
I'm told to clean my room; it's such a bore,
I say there really is no point at all,
They don't listen to me anymore,
It is as if I'm talking to a wall.
Soon I'll be starting university,
Of course my parents think that they know best,
They want to make me go off to Dundee,
Though Liverpool is better than the rest.
But now, I see as I write this short rhyme,
My parents do know best, most of the time.

Emma Shakeshaft (13)
Polam Hall School

Dreams

What are the dreams we dreamers dream each night,
The weird thoughts at the back of every brain?
Are they the way we try to get life right?
For all the dreams that I have are insane.
What are the stupid things that we call dreams,
The visions we all have when we're in bed,
Where nothing ever is quite what it seems,
Where everything stays one unfinished thread?
What if it's not our dreams that are unreal,
But when we are awake that we're deceived?
In dreams is what we really see and feel,
In dreams are all the things to be believed,
So when we do things in our conscious mind,
We cannot ever know what lies behind.

Harriet Bradshaw (13)
Polam Hall School

Morning

What is it that makes mornings such a drag?
There is no sound or movement on the roads
No life, no action - I don't mean to nag
But they just suck; I really hate them loads
You feel so warm and cosy in your bed
Why do you have to get up anyway?
The sound of buzzers ringing in your head
I have so much to do, so much to say
I should do what I want, I'm only young
But no one listens to a word I've said
And work is boring and school is no fun
But why can't I just jump out of this bed?
Is it for warmth and comfort that I stay
Or am I just too scared to face the day?

Sophie Villiers (13)
Polam Hall School

Sweetcorn

Sweetcorn is very nice
but it's nothing like rice
Sweetcorn is not my favourite
but I don't hate it
People think it's lazy
but I think it's as fresh as a daisy
When it's in your mouth
you know it; going south
When it goes down your throat
there's so much, it feels like a boat
When it's in your belly
it feels like a welly
Because it makes you so full
you feel fat like a bull
When you lie in the sun
it's a good job, as you're so full, you will not be able to run
When you are no longer full
you will be as skinny as a seagull.

Liam Wilson (14)
St Leonard's RC Comprehensive School, Durham

Christopher's Poem

My sweet little cherub it had to be,
The angels came to take you from me.
In my arms you lay that day,
When they took your hand and led you away.
We gave you our love, that's all we could do,
It's time to say goodnight to you.
So with many tears and a special prayer,
Pray Lord keep him in your care.

Gentle Jesus in Heaven above,
Please give Christopher all our love,
Keep him in your tender care,
And someday we will meet him there.

Stephen Small (13)
St Leonard's RC Comprehensive School, Durham

Tuna Fish

Tuna fish is a tasty dish,
You eat it how you like,
You can eat it when you wish.

You can eat it with salad,
You can eat it with chips,
Don't forget you have to wash your dish.

Some people like it,
Some people hate it,
I suppose that's the way we have to take it.

Emma Jackson (14)
St Leonard's RC Comprehensive School, Durham

A Teacher From Hell

There once was a teacher from Hell
Who had an incredible smell
Her bark was so strong
And her breath made such a pong
That the head teacher didn't like her as well.

Gerard Dawson (13)
St Leonard's RC Comprehensive School, Durham

The Teacher From Heaven

Gently she speaks her every word,
Gently she works on every world.
Gentle and happy on every day,
Gently she sings when the children play.
Gently she says, 'No homework today.'
Gently the class shout, 'Hooray, hooray!'
Gently she says, 'I will see you on Monday.'

Danilo Campoli (13)
St Leonard's RC Comprehensive School, Durham

Food

Everybody needs to eat,
to be alive and on their feet.
Food is good, food is great,
I eat my tea at a quarter to 8.
I never go without my lunch,
so give me something I can munch.
Set me free, let me be
let's sit down and have some tea.

Anthony Davison (14)
St Leonard's RC Comprehensive School, Durham

Food, Good And Bad

Pizza, burgers and chips are so salty,
These things they say
Will make your heart faulty.
As will sausages wrapped in a warm pastry,
It's a pity these foods are so tasty.
More apples, pears and grapes we should eat,
But a burger is great for a bit of a treat.

Jessica Longstaff (14)
St Leonard's RC Comprehensive School, Durham

The Teacher From Heaven

H eaven is where all nice teachers come from,
E vil ones come from Hell.
A ll helpful teachers are good,
V ery nice ones are great.
E very teacher should be helpful and nice,
N ot nasty or a bully.

Ross Spedding (13)
St Leonard's RC Comprehensive School, Durham

A Poem About Vegetables

Eat your vegetables
Clean your plate
Eat your vegetables
Veggies are great
String beans, broccoli
Lettuce and peas
Squash and Brussels sprouts
More corn please
Cucumbers, aubergine
Beets and tomatoes
Celery, carrots
Spinach and potatoes
Radishes, cauliflower
Cabbage and cress
Peppers and onions
Asparagus? Yes!
Black beans, red beans
Soya beans too
Eat your veggies
They're good for you!

Sarah Tracey (14)
St Leonard's RC Comprehensive School, Durham

Takeaway Foods

Indian takeaway smells so good,
Italian takeaway looks so good,
Chinese takeaway tastes so good,
But fish and chips just top the lot.

Too much choice I can never decide,
Oh please someone else decide,
I know in my mind what I will have to do,
Stomach the lot to be satisfied.

Craig Kelly (15)
St Leonard's RC Comprehensive School, Durham

M&Ms

When we eat our M&Ms
We eat the blue ones last
We suck them very slowly
We crunch them very fast.

When we eat our M&Ms
We nibble around the shell
We eat the chocolate then
We scoff them very well.

I eat sandwiches
Munch, munch, munch
I eat crisps
Crunch, crunch, crunch.

I eat lollies
Lick, lick, lick
But I eat my M&Ms
Quick, quick, quick.

Nickola Murphy (14)
St Leonard's RC Comprehensive School, Durham

Teacher From Hell

Have you seen him?
Have you? Have you?
He has moth-eaten scruffy clothes
He does! He does!

Have you heard him?
Have you? Have you?
Here come his big black boots,
Thump! Thump! Thump!

He enters fifteen minutes late,
'Detention! Detention!'

Sean Kelly (13)
St Leonard's RC Comprehensive School, Durham

Oh Roast Dinners

My favourite food is a dinner,
It is a Sunday roast,
It really is delicious,
And that's why I love it most.

The first thing that I do,
Is pick up the chicken,
It smells gorgeous and I know
So I give it a good licking.

I now move on to the big Yorkshire pudding,
It smells just as nice,
So I pick it up,
And bite into it twice.

Last but not least the roasties,
This is my favourite part,
They really are the nicest,
So eating them is an art.

I hope you enjoyed the poem,
The dinner has one more ingredient,
Here is a hint of what it is,
Northern boys love gravy.

Alan Devonport (14)
St Leonard's RC Comprehensive School, Durham

The Teacher From Hell

There was an old man called Joe
He had a deformed toe
We think he was from Hell
He let off a bad smell
For a teacher he was bad
He was racist and sad
That evil old man called Joe.

Thomas Bradley (13)
St Leonard's RC Comprehensive School, Durham

10 Minutes Left

10 minutes left
Wriggling
Savouring the comfort
Does it have to end soon?

7 minutes left
Please stop time!
It's too soft and warm and comfy
And . . .

3 minutes left
Must attempt a last minute sleep
Screaming inside at my waste of napping time

0 minutes left
Bright bulb bellowing
Shouting at me

-5 minutes left
I'm asleep.

Jess Baldasera (15)
St Leonard's RC Comprehensive School, Durham

Life

Argh! Awake,
Morning, morning,
Bypass breakfast,
Moaning mother,
Ah, life.

Hurried homework,
Fighting friends,
Unsightly uniform,
Concrete casing,
Ah, life.

Charlotte Davies (15)
St Leonard's RC Comprehensive School, Durham

My Life . . .

My life . . .
Daily prick of a diabetic needle.

My life . . .
Morning brings blinding brightness.

My life . . .
Cut of the cold wind brings bright blood to the surface.

My life . . .
School with enforced wakefulness and rules.

My life . . .
Weekends are my true life.

My life . . .
Hating the bright bustle of society.

My life . . .

Christine Melvin (15)
St Leonard's RC Comprehensive School, Durham

A Life In The Day Of Poem

Alas the bane of my morning deprives me of another forty winks with a rude and obnoxious beep!

Another unfortunate weekday unfolds and my fugitive trousers are on the run again.

Now aware of the time, I make good of the vacant bathroom and proceed to vigorously brush my face and wash my teeth.

The satisfaction of packing my bag the night before strikes me as I head out of the door.

Baffled, my mother queries where I'm going on a Sunday.

Rollocks!

Philip Morris (15)
St Leonard's RC Comprehensive School, Durham

Inner Struggle

The ape like figure heaves from comfort
Into Hell, never to come back.

Drifting in and out,
The struggle continues.

Homework? What homework?
The struggle continues . . .

Lessons begin, a weight under my eyes
The struggle continues . . .

Yet another detention
The struggle continues . . .

Where have the years of innocence skipped off to?
The struggle continues . . .

Asleep again
The struggle ends.

James Smith (16)
St Leonard's RC Comprehensive School, Durham

Still Asleep

I wrestle myself out of my cosy nest,
Still asleep.
And scramble across the bedroom floor,
Still asleep.
I trudge to the kitchen and delve in the fridge,
Still asleep.
I doze at the bus stop and linger on the bus,
Still asleep.
I fumble down to the yard and meet my friends,
Still asleep.
The horn blasts for the start of school,
Now I'm awake!

Stephanie Hannah (15)
St Leonard's RC Comprehensive School, Durham

Lazy

Yawn.
Crawl out of bed. Asleep?
Yawn.
Ooze down the stairs. Awake?
Yawn.
Heave on clothes. Asleep?
Yawn.
Fall out of home. Awake?
Yawn.
Collapse into chair. Asleep?
Yawn.
Mumble to classmates. Awake?
Yawn.
Teacher taps shoulder. Asleep?
Yawn.
Not anymore.

Matt Stokoe (15)
St Leonard's RC Comprehensive School, Durham

Fabulous Dream

The luxurious red carpet stretches out before me,
I smile,
casually, coolly
at the paparazzi.
The crowd pushes closer and closer,
relentless as an incoming tide.
I'm a celebrity,
I'm the Prime Minister,
I'm an Olympic gold medalist.
I'm . . .
a regular Year Eleven schoolgirl,
torn from her fabulous dream,
by the foghorn that is her alarm clock.

Ruth Innes (15)
St Leonard's RC Comprehensive School, Durham

The Big School

Scabby knees have faded now.
- like the paintings on the door.
The puddles on the yard are frozen
- like my presence in one time.
Winter days bring coats and scarves
- a metal box pulls me away.
I'm forced to go to big school
- nothing will ever be the same again.

Anna Craig (15)
St Leonard's RC Comprehensive School, Durham

Why Not?

I'm not even learning much!
Ink smudged across the page
I'm wasting my life in a classroom
Mind is elsewhere
What use will it be later?
More and more notes to copy
Why am I here?
But then again, why not?

Laura Armstrong (15)
St Leonard's RC Comprehensive School, Durham

Untitled

Wake up! Wake up!
The cold air overwhelms me
Precise, repetitive and soothingly loud
My consciousness strikes me
Have you seen the time?
The tranquil world of dreams shattered.

Arthika Sripathy (15)
St Leonard's RC Comprehensive School, Durham

A Trial Of Endurance: A Life In My Day

Back to the twilight zone
I stumble
Hair in eyes
Guided by early morning ESP.

Dressing, breakfast
Pack my bag
Bump-starting the car
Doesn't bump-start me.

First lesson
Seconds drag
With leaden heavy feet
Until the bell goes.

School passes
Pulling itself along on
The broken limbs
Of my no longer self-motivation.

The river, hazy in autumn mist
A trial of endurance
As the blades roll themselves
Between my frosty fingers.

A trial of endurance
That I feel I can never triumph
Never galloping home on my charger
To eternal rest in Avalon.

Meghan McCarthy (15)
St Leonard's RC Comprehensive School, Durham

The Teacher From Hell!

There once was a teacher from Hell,
Who gave off a really bad smell,
His voice was annoying,
And his lessons were boring,
That was the teacher from Hell.

Jonathan Todd (13)
St Leonard's RC Comprehensive School, Durham

Too Much

Too early, too awake,
Too alive.
Bus trip, mist and cold,
Too alive.
Blindness,
Winter frost, torturous rain,
Too alive.
Stiffness of clouds, cold air,
Shivers,
Too alive.
Friends, enemies, teachers,
Strangers,
Too alive.
Lessons,
Too alive.
School,
Again . . .

Emma Crilley (15)
St Leonard's RC Comprehensive School, Durham

Athletics!

I love athletics, it is fun,
Playing good sports in the sun,
You can make new friends,
And enjoy having new trends,
Sprinting is the best,
Better than all the rest.

Throwing and jumping are cool too,
Anybody can do it, all the way through,
I love athletics, it is great,
You can play or commentate.

Laura Burnip (13)
St Leonard's RC Comprehensive School, Durham

Ode To The School Bus

School bus, mental asylum - where is the blur?
Spitting Kate
Girl shake ties
Hedgehog look-alike
Radio advert sing along
I spy tree, tree, tree
A place where sanity dares not stray
School bus, mental asylum?
Mental asylum.

Yvonne Zhang (15)
St Leonard's RC Comprehensive School, Durham

A Rude Awakening

Creak, creak, bang
Evil face and evil mind
Creak, creak, shout
Evil morning and evil time
Creak, creak, giggle
Evil done, evil finished
Creak, creak, yawn
Evil is my little brother.

Stefanie Castellanos (15)
St Leonard's RC Comprehensive School, Durham

Heaven

H is for harmony
E is for everlasting life
A is for angels
V is for valour
E is for exile
N is for the newborn.

Amy Cooke (13)
St Leonard's RC Comprehensive School, Durham

Never Alone

Parties, gatherings, excitement
With my family you are never alone
Mad, witty, loving
With my family you are never alone
Fancy dress, squeals of laughter
With my family you are never alone
Suffocating venues with our masses
With my family you are never alone
Twenty-six of us ensures that
With my family you are never alone
But my family will make sure that
No one, no venue, no celebration, no idea will be left alone.

Sarah Churlish (15)
St Leonard's RC Comprehensive School, Durham

Poem

My teacher was sent from Heaven,
Her name is Mrs Bevil.
She's so kind you would think she's our mother,
We think she's great, some people want to be her lover.
We never get any homework,
We get all of our work finished in class.
Bevil never screams or stamps her feet,
She always says, 'All that will happen is that it will raise
                                      my blood pressure!'
She has some rules to keep the order,
But still Bevil is the best teacher in the nest.

Emma Bird (13)
St Leonard's RC Comprehensive School, Durham

Teacher From Hell!

The constant tapping,
Fingernails tapping on the desk,
The smell of her dreadful perfume,
The way her hair was scraped back with pins,
The red-gashed lipstick that smothered her lips,
The crooked teeth that were shown when she spoke,
The way her high heels tapped along the floor,
The way she cackled instead of laughed,
The teacher I don't want next year!

Marissa Morgan (13)
St Leonard's RC Comprehensive School, Durham

Our World

A dove is a sign of peace and love
He flies so gracefully in the sky up above
His soft white feathers make his soul free
I hope the dove brings peace to you and me.

A lion is a sweet animal on the inside
But angry on the outside
How would you feel locked up all day
With nothing to do but think and pray.

Certain people watch certain things
They watch you take your first step into this world
They watch you take your last step into their world
But one thing we do know is that they look after you.

These are your guardian angels.

Jessica Richardson & Natalie O'Connor
Spennymoor Comprehensive School

Care

Why am I in care
Is it because I have no friends
Or is it just because of me?

I had no one to talk to
Not my teachers, not my friends
The teachers thought it was not as bad as I made out
However, it was and I am the only one to know.

I never mixed in with other people
I used to stand out and be the class clown
With the other people making rude remarks.

Why me, why always me?
Does anybody love me?
Mum, come and save me.

Rebecca McKenzie
Spennymoor Comprehensive School